Contents

Fox Kids Hits 6

Ninja Turtles -
They're lean, green and teen 8

X-men 18

Monster Rancher -
The mystery of the disk 24

Princess Sissi -
Sissi's Teardrops 26

Digimon 40

Ace Ventura 64

Power Rangers Lost Galaxy 76

Sailor Moon 78

Spiderman 82

Ninja Turtles 94

X-men 102

Fox Kids Web page..................108

FOX KIDS™

Annual 2001

Pedigree

Pedigree Books Limited
The Old Rectory, Matford Lane, Exeter EX2 4PS
Published in 2000

Published by Pedigree Books Limited under licence from Fox Kids.

£6.99

FOX KIDS

Once you've finished all the puzzles and read all the stories in this annual then it'll be time to turn on Fox Kids and tune in to some of the coolest, funniest, most exciting shows on your TV.

If it's action that you're after then you can't beat **Power Rangers Lost Galaxy**. Get ready for intergalactic adventures with five of the coolest space warriors on TV.

The latest in the Power Rangers adventure series and this time the threat is galaxy wide. Tune in to help Leo, Kai, Kendrix, Damon and Maya in their quest to save the galaxy from Scorpius' evil powers. There are mysteries to be solved, questions to be answered and battles to be fought. The Power Rangers are committed to fighting evil but first they have to find out who's on their side.

If you'd rather tune into magic and mystery than intergalactic battles then **Mystic Knights of Tir Na Nog** will get your imagination racing. Set in a mythical time, long ago and far away Mystic Knights of Tir Na Nog will introduce you to a world where nothing is as it seems and everything has a hidden meaning.

Join Rohan, Angus, Deirdre and Ivar as they struggle to defeat the evil Queen Maeve and bring peace to their island. Bestowed with mysterious special powers and the strength of friendship this mixed bunch of princess and thief, mysterious foreigner and orphan forge their way in this world of magic, mythology and mystery.

Fox Kids isn't all about fighting evil and saving the world. When you meet **The New Addams Family** you'll realise there's more to life than fighting, and more to death than being buried. They're sticking around to make sure that Fox Kids stays as crazy and creepy as ever, and to teach us about how family life should be. This weird and wonderful family get their kicks from the strangest things, but don't be scared - they won't eat you!

Invite yourself round for tea and get to know Morticia, Fester, Lurch and Thing - but if you make friends with Wednesday and Pugsley you might get more than you bargained for...

One for the girls...

You might think that Fox Kids is mainly for boys but we've got some great shows for girls too. **Princess Sissi** comes top in the romance stakes, but she's not just a pretty face. A strong, independent, feisty girl - Sissi's not going to let anything come between her and the prince. Based on a true story this show is guaranteed to make your heart flutter, it's proof that fairy tales really do happen.

You might think that you don't want to watch a soppy love story but Sissi has her fair share of adventures as she fights to get her Prince and keep her family together.

Hits

They're lean, green and teen...

Remember 1987? Of course you don't! Before your time, wasn't it? Well, it was a very special year. Britain and America were both struck by powerful forces! On this side of the Atlantic, a mighty hurricane swept across the country, flattening everything in its path. And, in New York, the streets were hit by an even greater whirlwind - Leonardo, Raphael, Donatello and Michaelangelo - the Teenage Mutant Ninja Turtles!

Splinter

The exploits of these four, battling deadly villains like The Shredder, have become the stuff of legend. But time has moved on and the Turtles have grown older and wiser. They have fully learned The Way Of The Body And The Fist (which they call: "The Way Of The Turtle - mess with green and things get mean!") and are ready to face a new challenge. And that is literally just around the corner!

Donatello

Leornardo

Michaelangelo

Raphael

Venus

New York today faces a new and terrible threat. The Dragon Lord, along with his brutal troops called The Rank, have escaped from the magical Dragon Prison and plan to take over the Earth. As if this wasn't enough, the wicked Dragon Lord also wants the powers of the Turtles for himself!

This time, however, the famous foursome have help in their struggle against the forces of evil. A fifth fighter has joined their ranks... a female turtle! Unknown to them, on that fateful day so long ago, another Turtle had fallen out of the jar and into the sewer. Found by a Chinese wise man called Chung I, the young girl Turtle was taken back to China and brought up in the ancient way of the Mind and Spirit rather than the Ninja way of the Body and Fist.

Now reunited with the four Ninja Turtles under the manhole cover in New York's Lower East Side, Venus (as she is nicknamed) adds her special skills to the battle against the Dragon Lord. Only these five, and their ever-patient guide Splinter, stand between us and the end of the world as we know it.

The teenage Mutant Ninja Turtles are back!

Cowabunga!

The Dragon Lord

FOX KIDS™

PATHETIC FOOLS! USE YOUR **BRAINS** – IF YOU HAVE ANY – TO **THINK**! TAKE THE TURTLES BY **SURPRISE**!
LOOK, BEBOP – MUTAGEN! OLD SHREDHEAD TREATS WHAT'S LEFT OF THAT GOO LIKE GOLD-DUST! IT'S REAL POWERFUL!
LET'S SEE WHAT HAPPENS IF WE POUR SOME OVER DEM TURTLES!
MUTAGEN
LOOK WHO'S COMIN', GUYS!
THOSE GEEKS BEBOP AND ROCKSTEADY!
I WISH ALL THE BAD GUYS WE MEET UP WITH WERE AS STUPID AS THOSE TWO!
I TELL YA, WE'RE GONNA GIVE THOSE TURTLES THE SHOCK OF THEIR LIVES...
YEAH! WE'LL MAKE 'EM **JUMP**–!
MUTAGEN
BOOOOO!
YAAAAAAAH!
EEEEEK!

OKAY, GUYS — LET'S SORT 'EM OUT !
YAAARGH !
UUURRRGH !
HAVE A NICE DAY, GEEKS !
WE'RE STUPID!
AT THAT MOMENT, OUT IN SPACE...
THE FLEET OF GALACTIC TRANSPORTERS ARE FROM AN EXPERIMENTAL BREEDING FARM...
ALARM ! STEERING BEAM OUT OF ALIGNMENT ! I AM LOSING CONTROL !

TWO SPACE CRAFT COLLIDE !
KLUNNKK !
A SOLITARY PIECE OF CARGO IS DISLODGED...
...THE EGG FALLS TOWARDS NEW YORK CITY...
THE SHELL OF THE GALACTIC EGG IS MADE OF IMPERVIOUS CARBONITE...
IT HEADS FOR THE SAME SEWER GRATING THAT THE TURTLES THEMSELVES ONCE FELL THROUGH...
CRASH!
AND NOW, WAITING BELOW...THE FORGOTTEN CONTAINER OF MUTAGEN...
MUTAGEN

WHAT WAS THAT ?
SOUNDED LIKE A SPLASH... IN THE NEXT CHAMBER !
GRAB YOUR WEAPONS, GUYS !
THEY ARE JUST IN TIME TO WITNESS A STARTLING TRANSFORMATION !
IT'S AN EGG !
AND GETTING BIGGER BY THE SECOND !
TUBULAR !
CRAAACCCKKK !
GUURRKK ?
WH-WHAT THE PERISHIN' PIZZA IS THAT ?
A WEIRDO !
A LITTLE DRAGON !
HIYA, FELLER ! WHERE DID YOU COME FROM ?
HOW ABOUT DRAGON-LAND !
SUDDENLY...
A FIRE BREATHER ! KNOCK IT OFF, PAL !
WHOOOSSHH !
WE PREFER COOL DUDES !

THEN...
HE'S CLIMBING OUT OF THE SEWER!
YOU CAN'T GO UP THERE...
HE CAN! HE'S DONE IT! WE'VE GOTTA GET HIM BACK!
AAAAAAAH! WHAT IS IT!
A WALKING FIRE-LIGHTER!
HELP!
STORE
HE'S HEADIN' FOR THAT WAREHOUSE!
AFTER HIM, BROTHERS! HAUL SHELL!
BUT AS THEY ROUND A CORNER...
WAY OUT!
WOW!
MONDO BIZARRO!
DIG THAT!
IT'S SHREDHEAD AND HIS MUTANTS!
THEY MUST HAVE BEEN USING THE WAREHOUSE AS A TEMPORARY HEADQUARTERS!

INSIDE THE BUILDING...
LOOK WHAT I SEE!
ANTI-MUTAGEN!
ANTI-MUTAGEN
IF MUTAGEN MAKES YOU BIG...ANTI-MUTAGEN MUST MAKE YOU SMALL!
GUYS, I GOT AN IDEA! TURTLES LIKE PIZZA... PERHAPS DRAGONS DO AS WELL!
TEN MINUTES LATER...
HERE HE COMES! KEEP DOWN!
HE'S SNIFFING! HE CAN SMELL THE PIZZA!
SO CAN I — AND IT MAKES ME HUNGRY!
GET READY WITH THAT SPRAY OF ANTI-MUTAGEN, DON!
CHOMP!
CHOMP!
CHOMP!
NOW! HAVE SOME ANTI-MUTAGEN, FELLA!

UURRKKK !
IT'S WORKING !
HE'S SHRINKING BACK TO HIS EGG SIZE !
A SUDDEN, BLINDING FLASH OF LIGHT !
HE - HE'S VANISHING !
...BEING BEAMED UP INTO SOME SORT OF SPACE CRAFT !
HE CAME FROM SPACE - NOW HE'S GOING BACK !
MAYBE IT'S FOR THE BEST, DUDES...
NEW YORK'S NOT READY FOR DRAGONS AS WELL AS TURTLES ! AT LEAST NOT YET !
COWABUNGA TO THAT !
DON'T FORGET TO BUY THE TURTLES COMIC EVERY FORTNIGHT !
END !

Eek! STRAVAGANZA™
© & TM 1992
Fox Children's Network Inc.
SCREAM
WAIL!
SOUNDS LIKE SOMEONE'S IN TROUBLE.......
ANOTHER JOB FOR....
SUPEREEK
I BAPTISE THIS CHILD ..... YEOUW !
SNATCH
!
YOU TAKE THE KID, I'LL HOLD THE GUY IN THE DRESS !
THANKS TO YOU, MY CHILD HAS BEEN CHRISTENED YEOUW !
ERRR !
YEOUW - MMM... IT'S QUITE A NICE NAME REALLY...
SPLAT!
YEOUW !
SOMEONE CALLED ?
MM98

HOME TO RENT
STEREO
BUD
GORGIOUS
CANDY
ETNO
OH MY MUSHROOM. HOW I LOVE YOU!
BUD HAS FALLEN FOR FUNGI AGAIN!
WHAT A LOVELY CAP YOU HAVE
WHAT IS THIS FIXATION FOR FUNGOID FORMS BUD HAS?
COME AND WATCH T.V. WITH ME...I'LL FETCH YOU A CUSHION
HM!!
TOSS
AAGGHH!!! WHERE IS MY MUSHROOM?
GORGIOUS HAS HELPED YOU WITH SOME DEPRIVATION THERAPY BUD!
YOU'VE EATEN IT GORGIOUS HAVEN'T YOU?

STAN LEE PRESENTS: **CYCLOPS** WITH HIS OPTIC BLAST, **WOLVERINE** WITH HIS ADAMANTIUM CLAWS, AND **STORM** WITH HER POWER TO CONTROL THE WEATHER—TOGETHER WITH **ROGUE**, **GAMBIT**, **JUBILEE**, **BEAST**, AND **JEAN GREY**—THEY FORM A TEAM OF MUTANTS WHO USE THEIR INCREDIBLE POWERS TO FIGHT FOR PEACEFUL CO-EXISTENCE WITH HUMANITY. LED BY THE TELEPATH **PROFESSOR X**, THEY ARE THE. . .

X-MEN

HEY, YOU GUYS--COME BACK!
I WASN'T GOING TO HURT YOU!
IT'S YOUR OLD FRIEND--JUBILEE! DON'T YOU REMEMBER ME??
GET OUT OF OUR YARD, MUTANT!
JUBILEE, THEY DON'T KNOW WHAT THEY'RE SAYING!
YES THEY DO, STORM!
IF THEY'RE THAT STUPID, WHO NEEDS THEM?
BUT BEFORE I GO, I WANT TO LEAVE THEM SOMETHING TO REMEMBER ME BY!
BECAUSE I'M SURE GOING TO HAVE A HARD TIME FORGETTING ABOUT THEM.
I'LL USE MY POWERS TO FREEZE YOUR MARK IN THE SNOW, CHILD!
MAYBE IT WILL GIVE YOUR FRIENDS SOMETHING TO THINK ABOUT!
WOW!
LOOK AT THE PRETTY SNOW ANGEL!

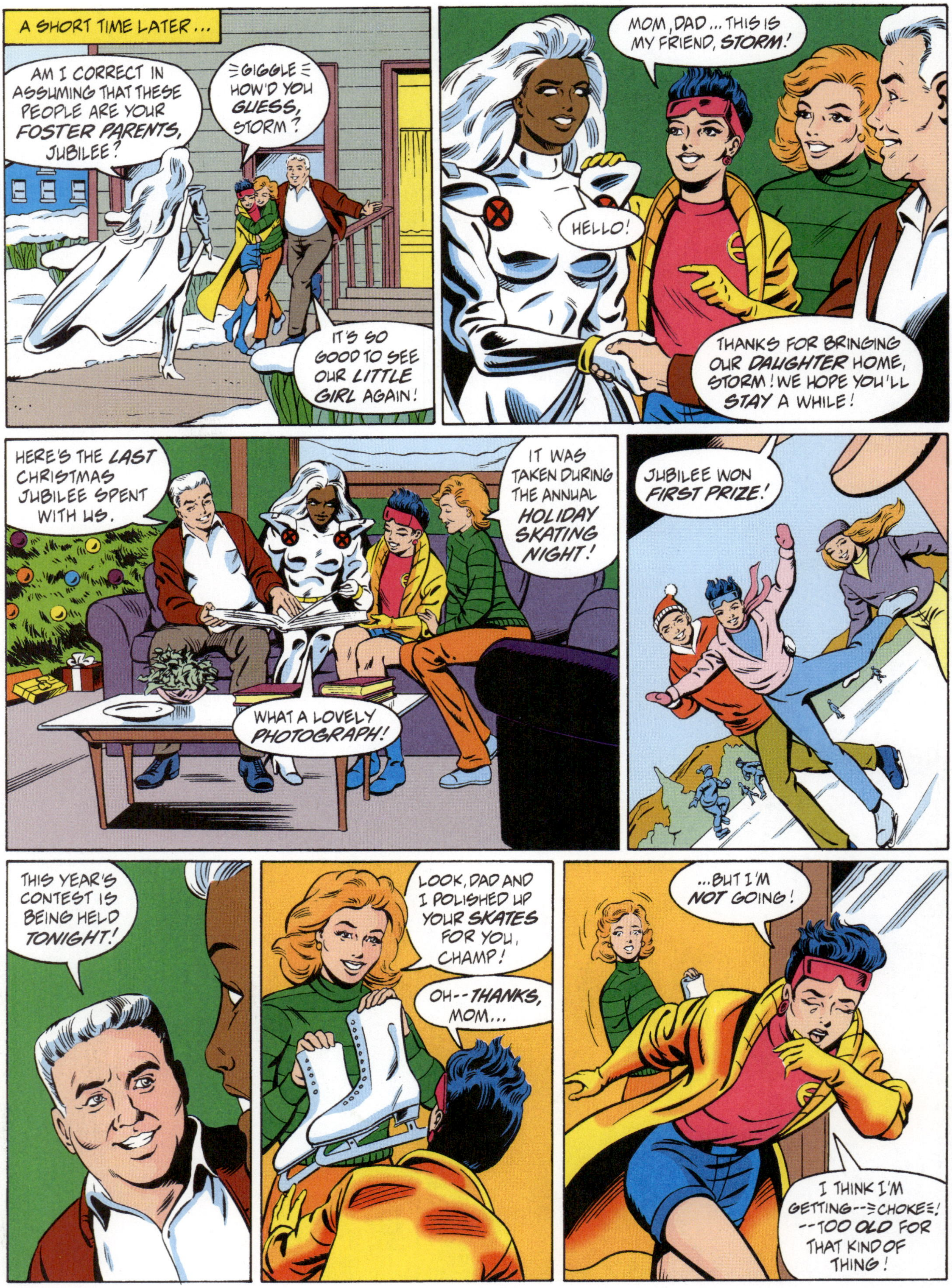
A SHORT TIME LATER...
AM I CORRECT IN ASSUMING THAT THESE PEOPLE ARE YOUR FOSTER PARENTS, JUBILEE?
=GIGGLE= HOW'D YOU GUESS, STORM?
IT'S SO GOOD TO SEE OUR LITTLE GIRL AGAIN!
MOM, DAD... THIS IS MY FRIEND, STORM!
HELLO!
THANKS FOR BRINGING OUR DAUGHTER HOME, STORM! WE HOPE YOU'LL STAY A WHILE!
HERE'S THE LAST CHRISTMAS JUBILEE SPENT WITH US.
IT WAS TAKEN DURING THE ANNUAL HOLIDAY SKATING NIGHT!
WHAT A LOVELY PHOTOGRAPH!
JUBILEE WON FIRST PRIZE!
THIS YEAR'S CONTEST IS BEING HELD TONIGHT!
LOOK, DAD AND I POLISHED UP YOUR SKATES FOR YOU, CHAMP!
OH--THANKS, MOM...
...BUT I'M NOT GOING!
I THINK I'M GETTING--=CHOKE=! --TOO OLD FOR THAT KIND OF THING!

LATER THAT NIGHT...
AS A MUTANT, I KNOW I WON'T BE WELCOME AT THE HOLIDAY SKATING NIGHT...
...BUT IT CAN'T HURT TO SNEAK DOWN AND TAKE A LOOK!
GEE... EVERYBODY SURE IS HAVING A GREAT TIME!
AND THEY DON'T MISS ME AT ALL!
CRIKK
HUH? WHAT'S THAT SOUND??
CRAACK
OH! HELP!
HOLY COW! THAT LITTLE GIRL'S IN BIG TROUBLE--
--AND EVERYONE ELSE IS HAVING TOO GOOD A TIME TO NOTICE!
DANGER THIN ICE
CRUNNCH
SNAP
PLEASE HELP ME!
THE CURRENT IS CARRYING HER AWAY!
NUTS! THIS BRANCH IS TOO SHORT!
I CAN'T REACH IT!

HMMM. I BET THIS TREE WOULD REACH HER...
I'LL JUST USE MY PLASMA BLAST TO MAKE LIKE A LUMBERJACK!
WHOOM
TIMBERRRR!
SPLASHH
I'VE GOT YOU, HONEY!
OH, THANK YOU!
WATCH YOUR STEP! THE GROUND IS VERY--
--SLIPPERY!
YOW! WAY TO TAKE YOUR OWN ADVICE, JUBILEE!
HEY, HOW COME THE WATER JUST TURNED TO ICE BENEATH ME??
STORM!
I COULDN'T LET YOU BE SWEPT AWAY, COULD I, CHILD?
RACHAEL!
UH-OH! WE'D BETTER SCRAM BEFORE THOSE MUTANT-HATERS SEE US, STORM!
WE FOUND RACHAEL!
MY BABY!

ARE YOU OKAY, RACHAEL?
YES, DADDY! THE ANGEL LADY SAVED ME!
HEY, LOOK!
IT'S A SNOW ANGEL!
FROZEN SOLID--JUST LIKE THE ONE JUBILEE MADE IN OUR FRONT YARD!
MINUTES LATER...
HUH? WHAT'S EVERYBODY DOING HERE, DAD??
THEY WANT TO THANK YOU, SWEETHEART!
WE KNOW THAT IT WAS YOU WHO SAVED OUR LITTLE GIRL!
THANK YOU, JUBILEE. YOU GAVE US THE BEST CHRISTMAS PRESENT IN THE WORLD!
I'M...JUST GLAD I COULD HELP.
FWUT
HUH?
HEY, JUBILEE!
WE WANT TO THANK YOU, TOO!
YEAH, BUT FIRST WE OWE YOU FOR THAT SNOWBALL YOU THREW AT US THIS AFTERNOON!
ALL RIGHT! THIS IS MORE LIKE IT!
I BELIEVE SHE'S FINALLY HOME!
THE END

Welcome to Fox Kids'

Monster Rancher

Here's what you need to know...

Genki, an 11 year-old computer whizz-kid, wins the final of the 'Monster Rancher' computer game competition and becomes national champion. As his grand prize, he is sent a 'Monster Rancher 200Z' CD-ROM. But when he starts to play his new game and generate a monster, something very strange happens. He finds himself transported into the 'Monster Rancher' world!

In this mysterious place, Genki meets a girl called Holly and a freindly, eyeball-shaped creature called Suezo. They are on the run from a group of evil monster who want to catch them. Genki joins his new friends as they make their escape.

Holly explains to Genki that all is not well in 'Monster Rancher' world. An elusive and wicked monster called Moo has taken over and wants to turn all the monsters in this world into evil ones. Only The Phoenix, which is sleeping in a special "Disk", can stop this and turn the monsters back into good ones. So Holly and Suezo are

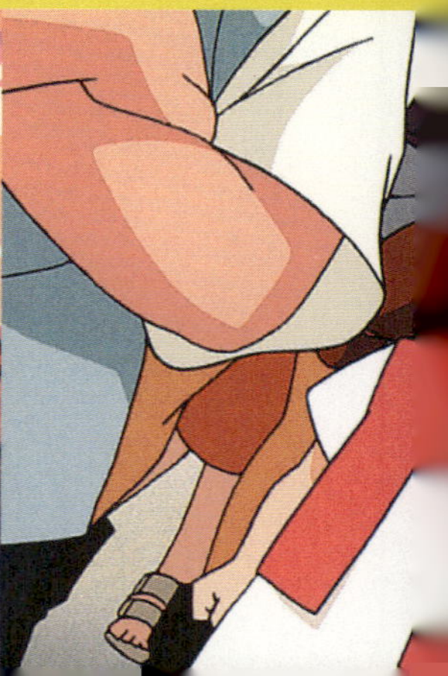

ensational new series...

The Mystery of The Disk

on a mission to find The Disk before Moo and his wicked friends can stop them.

Genki joins their quest, revealing the special CD-ROM that he won in the competition.. Holly is very excited, believing this could be what they are looking for, but it does not turn out that way. Instead of generating The Phoenix, Genki's disc gives birth to a cute-looking pink monster called Mocchi!

And so the dangerous journey begins. Picking up other friends like Tiger, Hare and the mighty Golem along the way, our young heroes enjoy one exciting adventure after another as they strive to find the "Disc" where the Phoenix is sleeping.

share in all the excitement and fun by watching 'Monster Rancher' on Fox Kids!

SABAN'S

Sissi

La Principessa • The Princess • La Princesse • La Princesa • die Prinzessin

Close your eyes and take yourself back in time to the wonderful unspoilt countryside of central Europe of 150 years ago... Sissi is a very beautiful 16 year old girl from the hills and mountains of southern Germany. One day, she meets a young man called Franz-Josef. He is handsome, gentle and kind. The couple fall in love at first sight. But how long will their fairy-tale romance last? Franz-Josef is a noble Prince and soon to become ruler of the mighty Austro-Hungarian Empire...

Did You Know...?

Sissi's story is based on a real-life person, Princess Elizabeth of Austria. Born on December 24, 1837, she was said to be the most beautiful young woman in the whole of Europe. When she met Franz-Josef in August 1853, he really fell in love with her. He married her in April 1854, making her Queen of Austria and, later, of Hungary too.

Spot the difference

Can you spot SIX DIFFERENCES between these two pictures of Sissi on a swing?

Being a rich and powerful prince, Franz-Josef's love for Sissi was frowned upon by his family. But the Prince is determined to marry his beloved Sissi and it seems that nothing - not even the war that soon separates them - can disturb the deep love that binds them together. Yet someone trusted by Franz-Josef, his own mother the Empress Sophia, hates Sissi and will do anything she can to oppose the wedding.

So what will happen? Find out as Sissi faces the horrors and disruption of war, powerful enemies and months of lonely separation from her Prince as she strives to make their love triumph in the end.

FOX KIDS™

SABAN'S Sissi
La Principessa • The Princess • La Princesse • La Princesa • die Prinzessin

Sissi's Teardrops

I'M IN LOVE, MUM. I DID WANT YOU TO BE THE FIRST ONE TO KNOW THAT!
THAT'S WONDERFUL! AND WHO WOULD BE THIS SO LUCKY MAN? IS IT SOMEBODY WE KNOW?
DON'T ASK ME QUESTIONS RIGHT NOW. WHEN DAD WILL BE HERE I'LL TELL YOU THE WHOLE STORY!
IN THE MEANTIME FRANZ IS COMING BACK TO THE PALACE TO SAY TO HIS MUM HE WANTS TO MARRY SISSI.
YOUR HIGHNESS, YOU ARE BACK!

WHERE IS MY MOTHER? I WANT TO SPEAK WITH HER RIGHT NOW!
SHE IS IN THE COUNCIL ROOM AND SHE IS WAITING FOR YOU.
HERE I AM, MOTHER.
FRANZ, THIS IS A SPECIAL MEETING. I HAVE TO TELL YOU ABOUT SOME IMPORTANT DECISIONS...
AS YOU KNOW YOU WILL SOON BE CROWNED AS EMPEROR OF AUSTRIA, THEREFORE IT IS TIME YOU FIND A WIFE...
WHAT A COINCIDENCE. I WAS JUST...
LET ME END MY SPEECH, FRANZ

AFTER A LONG CONSULTATION, THE CHAMBERLAIN AND ME AGREED THAT THE BEST WOMAN WHO COULD BECOME YOUR WIFE IS...
...HELEN!
WHAT?
I'M IN LOVE WITH SISSI! I'LL NEVER MARRY HELEN!
YOU'LL NEVER STOP ME FROM MARRYING SISSI!
SISSI? NEVER! THAT UNPOLISHED PEASANT WILL NEVER BE EMPRESS. HER FATHER EVEN GAVE SHELTER TO AN HUNGARIAN REBEL!

WHAT? YOU WANT TO MARRY FRANZ?
IN THE MEANTIME SISSI ALSO IS TELLING HER PARENTS THAT THE BOY SHE LOVES IS FRANZ...
I'LL NEVER ALLOW YOU TO MARRY THAT ENEMY OF THE HUNGARIAN PEOPLE!
FRANZ HAS NOTHING AGAINST HUNGARY AND I LOVE HIM ANYWAY AND I WANT TO MARRY HIM!
GO TO YOUR ROOM AND WAIT THERE UNTIL FURTHER ORDERS!
THAT'S SO CRUEL! YOU CANNOT STOP ME FROM MARRYING THE MAN I LOVE!

IN THE MEANTIME AT THE IMPERIAL PALACE...
OH MY BELOVED QUEEN, WHATEVER I DID TO DESERVE SUCH A TREATMENT FROM YOUR SON!
YOU CAN STOP PRETENDING THAT WAY...
...I REFUSE TO MARRY HELEN. AND THAT'S ALL!
YOU WERE LOOKING FOR ME, YOUR MAJESTY.
YES, COUNCILLOR, IT SEEMS THAT THIS TIME, FRANZ DON'T WANT TO LISTEN TO ME...

FRANZ WANT TO MARRY SISSI AT ANY PRICE.
EVEN IF THE BOY SEEMS TO BE SO FIRM I'VE GOT A PLAN TO CONVINCE HIM TO MARRY MISS HELEN...
THAT'S WONDERFUL. TELL ME EVERYTHING!
IN THE MEANTIME, IN POSSI SISSI IS IN DESPAIR. ONLY TOMMY'S SYMPATHY, SEEMS TO BOOST HER MORALE...
COME ON SISSI. I NEVER SAW YOU SO SAD!

YOU ARE RIGHT, CRYING IS POINTLESS. I WANT TO GO TO SPEAK WITH FRANZ. TOGETHER WITH HIM I'LL BE ABLE TO PERSUADE MY FATHER...
GET READY, TOMMY, IT IS TIME TO LEAVE HOME AGAIN!
AT THAT VERY MOMENT FRANZ IS GOING TO BE THE VICTIM OF THE PLOT PLANNED BY HIS MOTHER AND ZOTTORNICK...
MOTHER, THEY TOLD ME RIGHT KNOW YOU ARE NOT FEELING WELL...
UNFORTUNATELY I'M ILL, MY SON! PERHAPS MY TIME HAS COME...

MOTHER, DON'T SAY THAT!
IN THIS MOMENT OF ANGUISH I WANT YOU TO PROMISE YOU WILL MARRY HELEN!
WHAT? I CAN'T, I...
THE QUEEN'S HEART CANNOT STAND MORE SORROWS...
OKAY, I SOLEMNY PROMISE I'LL MARRY HELEN!
THANK YOU, SON, TO KNOW YOUR DECISION MAKES ME FEEL BETTER.

SISSI IS STILL TRYING TO REACH HER BELOVED FRANZ KNOWING NOTHING. AS SHE WALKS THROUGH THE VILLAGE AN IMPORTANT STATEMENT FROM THE BURGOMASTER ATTRACTS HER ATTENTION.
DEAR CITIZENS, I'M HAPPY TO ANNOUNCE YOU THE EMPEROR FRANZ ANNOUNCED HIS WEEDING!
IT IS SO EXCITING! FRANZ HAS ANNOUNCED OUR WEEDING YET!
THE FUTURE EMPRESS OF AUSTRIA WILL BE HELEN, DUCHESS VON GROSSBERG!
WHAT? HELEN?
SISSI FAINTS AWAY. THAT NEWS GAVE HER SO MUCH PAIN! NOW SHE BELIEVES FRANZ DOES NOT LOVE HER ANYMORE!
The End

FOX KIDS network
Eek! STRAVAGANZA™
© & TM 1992
Fox Children's Network Inc.
THAT LADY'S CAR HAS BROKEN DOWN! THIS IS A-JOB FOR ....
CLUNK CLUNK!
SUPEREEK
JUST OPEN THE BONNET MADAM, WE SHALL SOON HAVE IT FIXED
AH,... MMM....TUT TUT... COULD BE A BIG JOB
JUST POP THIS OUT...
AND THIS...
MMM... AHA !
HERE'S THE PROBLEM, YOU'VE GOT A SCREW LOOSE!
I SUGGEST YOU JUST GET A GARAGE TO REPLACE THE SCREW AND GET THEM TO POP ALL THESE BITS BACK FOR YOU...
THERE'S NO PLEASING SOME PEOPLE....

FOX KIDS network
Eek! STRAVAGANZA™
© & TM 1992
Fox Children's Network Inc.
EEK AND SHARKEY ARE PLAYING COMPUTER GAMES WHEN...
THIS ROOM IS A MESS, CLEAN IT UP!
JUST THROW IT ALL IN THE WARDROBE SHARKEY
PHEW... TIDY AT LAST...
GREAT JOB EEK,
I JUST NEED TO GET SOMETHING FROM THE WARDROBE...
ERRR.......
THAT'S IT! I WANT ALL THIS STUFF THROWN IN THE RUBISH BIN
WHERE'S SHARKEY? I NEED HIM TO TAKE THESE SACKS TO THE BIN
HE'S BIN AND GONE!
I REFUSE! I REFUSE!
MM98

HOME TO RENT
STEREO
BUD
GORGIOUS
CANDY
ETNO
AND THIS SUMMER THERE WILL BE A TOTAL ECLIPSE OF THE SUN
ETNO. WHAT'S A TOTAL ECLIPSE OF THE SUN?
WELL BUD. IT'S A PHENOMENA THAT OCCURS WHEN THIS PLANETS MOON MOVES DIRECTLY IN FRONT OF THE SUN...CAUSING A HUGE SHADOW ON EARTH THAT APPARENTLY BLOTS IT OUT!! A VERY STRANGE CORONA EFFECT CAN BE OBSERVED!
A RARE OCCURRENCE BY ALL ACCOUNTS!
HUMANS GET QUITE EXCITED BY THE EVENT!
HUH!! THAT'S NOTHING...I KNOW OF ANOTHER EVEN RARER OCCURRENCE!
IT ONLY TAKES PLACE EVERY MILLION YEARS!!
AND WHAT IS IT?
A TOTAL RABBIT SHAPE OF THE MOON!

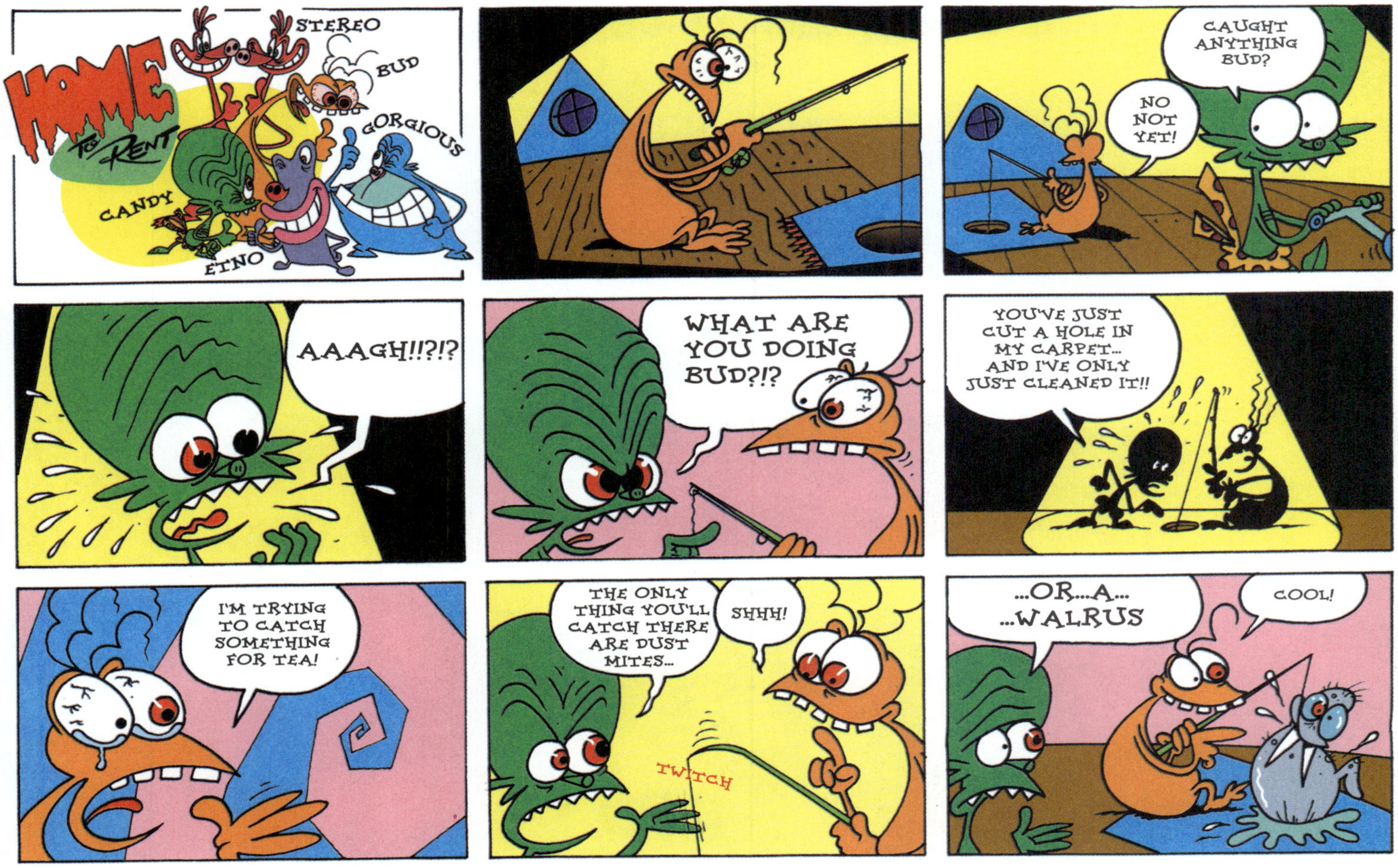
HOME TO RENT
STEREO
BUD
GORGIOUS
CANDY
ETNO
CAUGHT ANYTHING BUD?
NO NOT YET!
AAAGH!!?!?
WHAT ARE YOU DOING BUD?!?
YOU'VE JUST CUT A HOLE IN MY CARPET... AND I'VE ONLY JUST CLEANED IT!!
I'M TRYING TO CATCH SOMETHING FOR TEA!
THE ONLY THING YOU'LL CATCH THERE ARE DUST MITES...
SHHH!
TWITCH
...OR...A... ...WALRUS
COOL!

DIGITAL DIGIMON MONSTERS™

When seven children at Summer Camp are unexpectedly transported by alien digivices to the strange and dangerous planet known as DigiWorld, their lives are changed forever!

Tai, Sora, Izzy, Joe, Mimi, Matt and T.K. find themselves befriended by creatures known as Digimon, who, with the help of the digivices, can transform - digivolve! - into powerful digital monsters!

These Digimon protect the children against evil Digimon, while the children themselves are on a mission to save DigiWorld from an evil force that can turn good Digimon into bad Digimon!

TAI

Self-opinionated and loud, Tai is the leader of the group. Brave and athletic, he is determined to lead his friends home. His Rookie Digimon partner is Agumon.

SORA

The sensible one, Sora is calm and rational. She takes responsibility for keeping her friends safe. Her Rookie Digimon partner is Biyomon.

MATT

A born rebel, Matt tries to act cool in front of his friends, but he has a sensitive side he doesn't want anyone to see. His Rookie Digimon partner is Gabumon.

T.K.

T.K. is Matt`s younger brother. He hero-worships Matt and always tries to be brave in front of him. His Rookie Digimon partner is Patamon.

JOE

Joe is the worrier of the group. Scared of everything, he's the first to hide when trouble appears. His Rookie Digimon partner partner is Gomamon.

MIMI

Sweet and caring, but very fussy and self-centred, Mimi is completely out of place on DigiWorld. Her Rookie Digimon partner is Palmon.

IZZY

Izzy is a computer whizz-kid, who is so wrapped up in analysing everything he sees, he doesn't notice the danger around him. His Rookie Digimon partner is Tentamon.

KABUTERIMON'S ELECTRO SHOCKER!

GEEZ, YOU WOULD THINK I'M HURTIN' THE DUMB THING.
TOO BAD YOUR BRAIN ISN'T AS BIG AS YOUR HAIR MAYBE IZZY DOESN'T WANT GRIMY FINGERPRINTS AND DENTS ALL OVER HIS COMPUTER.
HMMPH.
DO YOU GUYS SEE SMOKE OVER THERE?
I'LL CHECK IT OUT.
HEY, TAI, WAIT FOR ME.
WHATEVER.
WE GOT GRAPHICS, WE GOT SOUND.
BEAUTIFUL! UP AND RUNNING. BUT THE BATTERY NEEDS RECHARGING.

GET OVER HERE, QUICK!
LOOKS LIKE SOME KIND OF FACTORY.
WHAT DO YOU SUPPOSE THEY MAKE IN THERE?
I DON'T KNOW, BUT WOULDN'T IT BE GREAT IF THERE'S A MANUFACTURER'S OUTLET STORE? THEY ALWAYS HAVE KILLER DEALS.
THERE DOESN'T SEEM TO BE ANYBODY HERE.
THERE'S GOTTA BE SOMEONE RUNNING THE EQUIPMENT.
IT APPEARS TO BE DOING QUITE WELL ALL BY ITSELF.
MATT, WHAT ARE THE MACHINES MAKING?
YOU GOT ME. MAYBE PARTS FOR ROBOTS OR SPACE SHIPS.
SOMEBODY'S GOTTA BE MOVIN' THOSE BELTS. AND PEOPLE GOTTA EAT, SO IS THERE A CAFETERIA IN THIS PLACE, 'CUZ WE COULD REALLY USE A GOOD MEAL!
WE CAN COVER MORE GROUND IF WE SPLIT UP...

HELLO?! IS ANYBODY HERE?!
WAIT A MINUTE. DON'T GO ANY FURTHER IN THIS DIRECTION.
WHAT IS IT, BIYOMON?
I'M NOT SURE. I HEARD SOMETHING.
SWOOSH...
CRUNCH
DOESN'T SOUND GOOD TO ME.
ELSEWHERE...
POWER SUPPLY R.
I SAY WE GO INSIDE AND HAVE A LOOK AROUND.
GASP!
DEADLINE
A BATTERY LIKE THAT COULD RUN MY COMPUTER FOREVER... I WONDER IF THERE'S A WAY TO ACCESS ITS POWER.

MEANWHILE...
HEY!
WHAT DO YOU SUPPOSE HAPPENED TO HIM?
WHO KNOWS, BUT LET'S SEE IF WE CAN HELP.
IT'S JUST A BUSTED ROBOT.
IT'S NOT A ROBOT. IT'S ANDROMON.
WHAT? THIS BIG KLUNK IS A DIGIMON?
YEAH, AND VERY ADVANCED.
POOR THING. I GUESS HE GOT CAUGHT IN THE GEARS AND GOT MANGLED.
MAYBE IF WE WORK TOGETHER, WE CAN PULL HIM OUTTA THERE.
MY MOM REALLY DOESN'T WANT ME MOVING ANY HEAVY OBJECTS. I'VE GOT BAD KNEES.
RELAX. WE'LL DO IT.
RIGHT!

I THINK IT'S MOVING!
UH?!
CLICK!
WHIR- WHIR- WHIR!
HEY! SOMETHING'S HAPPENING! HE'S COMIN' LOOSE.
YEAH!
I THINK HE'S SLOWLY COMING TO.

NOOO!
HE NEEDS A COUPLE OF WHACKS FOR A JUMP-START!
WHANG!
I AM ANDROMON...
I SAW A MOVIE ONCE WHERE A ROBOT CAME TO LIFE AND ATE EVERYBODY.
HE LOOKS FRIENDLY ENOUGH. I'M SURE IF WE'RE NICE TO HIM, HE'LL BE NICE TO US.
HUH?

FORGET WHAT I SAID ABOUT HIM BEING FRIENDLY!
I SHALL PUNISH ALIEN INTRUDERS.
LET'S GIVE HIM WHAT WE GOT!
SPIRAL TWISTER!
RAAAAGH!
UHG!

AGUMON, HOW ABOUT TRYING TO BLAST THE ROOF?
EEEEYAH!
SKREEE...
CRASH
UHHHH!
BOY, HE'S GONNA HAVE ONE UGLY HEADACHE.
NO DOUBT.
NOW, LET'S GET OUT OF HERE!

MEANWHILE...
WHAT YA DOIN', IZZY?
I'M TRYING TO TAP INTO THIS POWER SOURCE.
IF I CAN GET THIS BABY TO FIRE UP, WE CAN USE MY COMPUTER TO GET HELP.
AH-HA! I'VE LOCATED AN ACCESS PANEL TO THE INTERIOR OPERATIONS.
HEY, LET ME SEE, IZZY. WHAT EXACTLY DO YOU THINK THIS IS?
THESE MARKINGS ARE BINARY ANNOTATIONS OF SOME SORT, A COMPUTER PROGRAM.
A VERY COMPLICATED PROGRAM, INDEED.

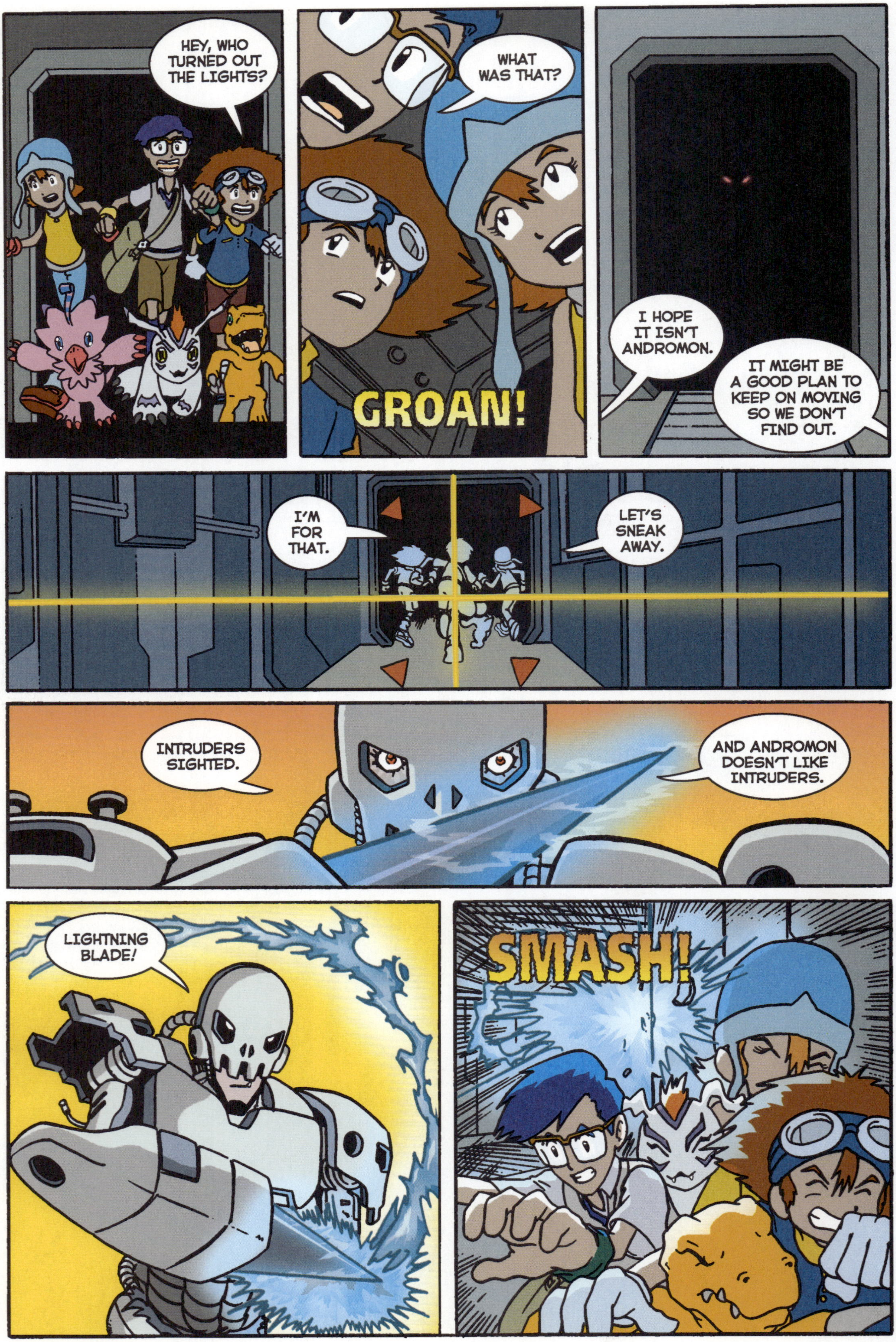
HEY, WHO TURNED OUT THE LIGHTS?
WHAT WAS THAT?
GROAN!
I HOPE IT ISN'T ANDROMON.
IT MIGHT BE A GOOD PLAN TO KEEP ON MOVING SO WE DON'T FIND OUT.
I'M FOR THAT.
LET'S SNEAK AWAY.
INTRUDERS SIGHTED.
AND ANDROMON DOESN'T LIKE INTRUDERS.
LIGHTNING BLADE!
SMASH!

BACK AT THE POWER ROOM...
COULD I HAVE DELETED THE WRONG PROGRAM?
I THINK THAT THAT'S A DISTINCT POSSIBILITY. WHY DON'T YOU TRY TO UN-DELETE IT?
GOOD IDEA.
A STROKE OF METALLIC PAINT RIGHT HERE...
I ADMIRE THE WAY YOU KEEP WORKING WHILE YOUR FRIENDS ARE OUT HAVING FUN. DON'T YOU EVER FEEL SORT OF LEFT OUT?
NOT AT ALL. I'M JUST TRYING TO DETERMINE HOW WE ALL GOT TO THIS PLACE.
AND I'D LIKE TO LEARN MORE ABOUT YOU DIGIMON, PERHAPS PROVE SOME OF MY THEORIES.
102 /* fwsc sample... coast creation*/
110 float s
120 while s (1 or s)=2
132 input "ration 1 to 2 "; s
142 endwhile
152 k= screen (e and i) = 4th
162 end
172 kw3 = screen fractional
182 rod/ rod1/ rod3/ float
192 r= read () * read () * read (D)
200 input "ration 1 or s) = 2
230 screen 1.3.4.5.
240 endd
THEORIES, THEORIES. WHAT'S THE BIG MYSTERY? I AM WHO I AM.
REALLY?
I SIMPLY CAN'T UNDERSTAND THIS PREOCCUPATION WITH WHO YOU ARE.

IS THERE SOME KIND OF DEEP DARK SECRET IN YOUR ORIGINS?
OH, WELL...
DON'T YOU THINK IT'S TIME WE TOLD IZZY THE TRUTH, DEAR?
NO. I'M AFRAID IF WE TOLD HIM NOW IT MIGHT BE TOO BIG A SHOCK.
I KNOW YOU'RE TRYING TO DO WHAT'S BEST, BUT I WORRY, ONCE HE FINDS OUT, HE'LL BE UPSET THAT WE DIDN'T TELL HIM SOONER.
HONEY, WE JUST CAN'T THINK ABOUT THAT NOW...
IZZY?! IZZY?!
HUH?! UH, WHAT DID YA SAY?
YOU WERE OFF IN ANOTHER WORLD.
I'M STARTING TO FEEL STRANGE...
TENTOMON TO IZZY -- ARE YOU READING ME?
THIS IS MERELY SPECULATION, BUT I BELIEVE I'VE STUMBLED ON TO SOMETHING MORE THAN JUST A COMPUTER GAME.
OH MY, IT'S GETTING HOT IN HERE. OW! OW! I'M BURNING UP. DO SOMETHING, QUICKLY! I'M BEING ZAPPED!
WHAT'S GOING ON? HEY!

OOH! OUCH! I CAN'T STAND IT! HELP!
HMM, IS IT SHORT-CIRCUITING?
OOH! EEE! MERCY! YIKES!
I'M DISCONNECTING THE POWER. NOW I MAY NEVER FIGURE THE MYSTERY OUT.
WHOOOOO...
WHAT HAPPENED TO MY DIGIVICE?
MEANWHILE, ON THE ROOF...
I REALLY, REALLY HOPE THEY DESIGNED IT WITH A DOOR!
I KNOW THIS DOESN'T MAKE ANY SENSE, BUT THIS ENTIRE FACTORY IS DESIGNED TO PUT THINGS TOGETHER AND THEN TAKE THEM APART.
WHO KNOWS!
IT'S BASED ON PERPETUAL MOTION. NOTHING EVER STOPS, OR LEAVES.
HEY, EVERYBODY! YOU'LL NEVER GUESS WHAT I JUST DISCOVERED?

WHAT'S UP?
WELL, THE COMPUTER PROGRAM OPERATING THIS FACTORY IS PRODUCING THE POWER TO KEEP IT GOING.
EVEN MORE INCREDIBLE, IN DIGIWORLD, BASIC DATA IS A LIVING, VIABLE SUBSTANCE. IT'S ALIVE...
HEY, GUYS! LISTEN UP!
WE GOTTA GET OUT OF HERE. NOW!
WHAT DO YOU MEAN, TAI?
CAPTURE INTRUDERS! SENSORS DETECT HOSTILITY.
BRING INTRUDERS INTO FIRING RANGE.
BRING MISSILES TO POSITION...

...AND FIRE!
HELP, MATT!
T.K.!
LOOK OUT!
GABUMON -- DIGIVOLVE TO -- GARURUMON!
OH, NO!
BA-BOOM!
AAAHHHH!
BAM-BAM-BAM-BAM-BAM!

AGUMON -- DIGIVOLVE TO -- GREYMON!
SWOOSH!
BOOM!
WHO CHALLENGES ANDROMON?
BUNGLING WEAKLINGS!

YOU PUNY ONES DARE TO CHALLENGE ME?
HE'S MORE POWERFUL THAN EITHER OF OUR DIGIMON!
MAYBE BECAUSE HE'S ALL MACHINE. IT'S ALMOST LIKE HE'S DIGIVOLVED FAR BEYOND THE OTHER DIGIMON.
IS IT POSSIBLE WE COULD LOSE?
SMASH!
TRY RE-ENTERING THAT PROGRAM THAT ACTIVATED YOUR DIGIVICE.
I BELIEVE THAT'S THE KEY TO MY DIGIVOLVING.
YES!
IT'S GOT TO WORK...
IF I CAN JUST RECALL THE EXACT SEQUENCE...
TENTOMON -- DIGIVOLVE TO -- KABUTERIMON!

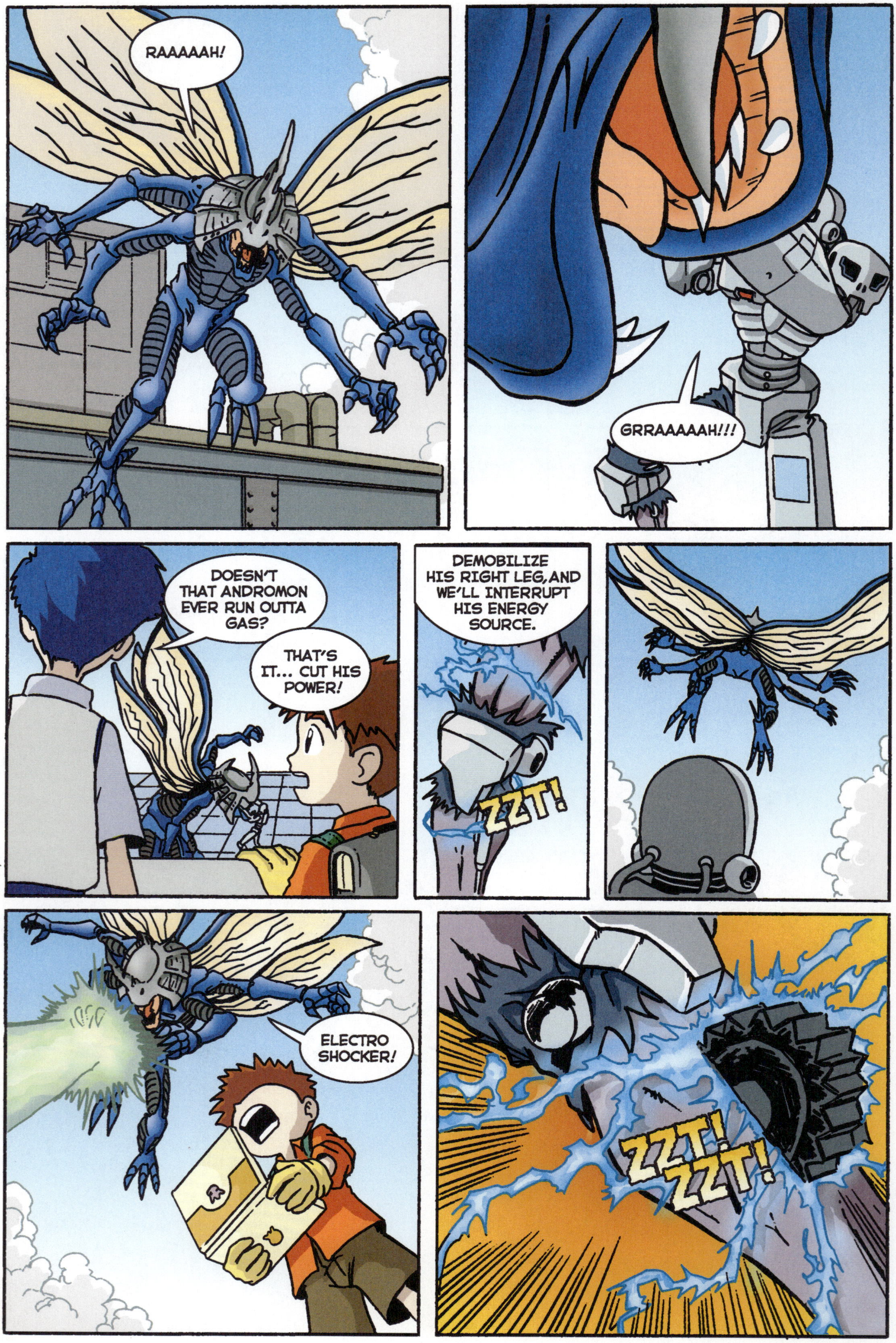
RAAAAAH!
GRRAAAAAH!!!
DOESN'T THAT ANDROMON EVER RUN OUTTA GAS?
THAT'S IT... CUT HIS POWER!
DEMOBILIZE HIS RIGHT LEG, AND WE'LL INTERRUPT HIS ENERGY SOURCE.
ZZT!
ELECTRO SHOCKER!
ZZT! ZZT!

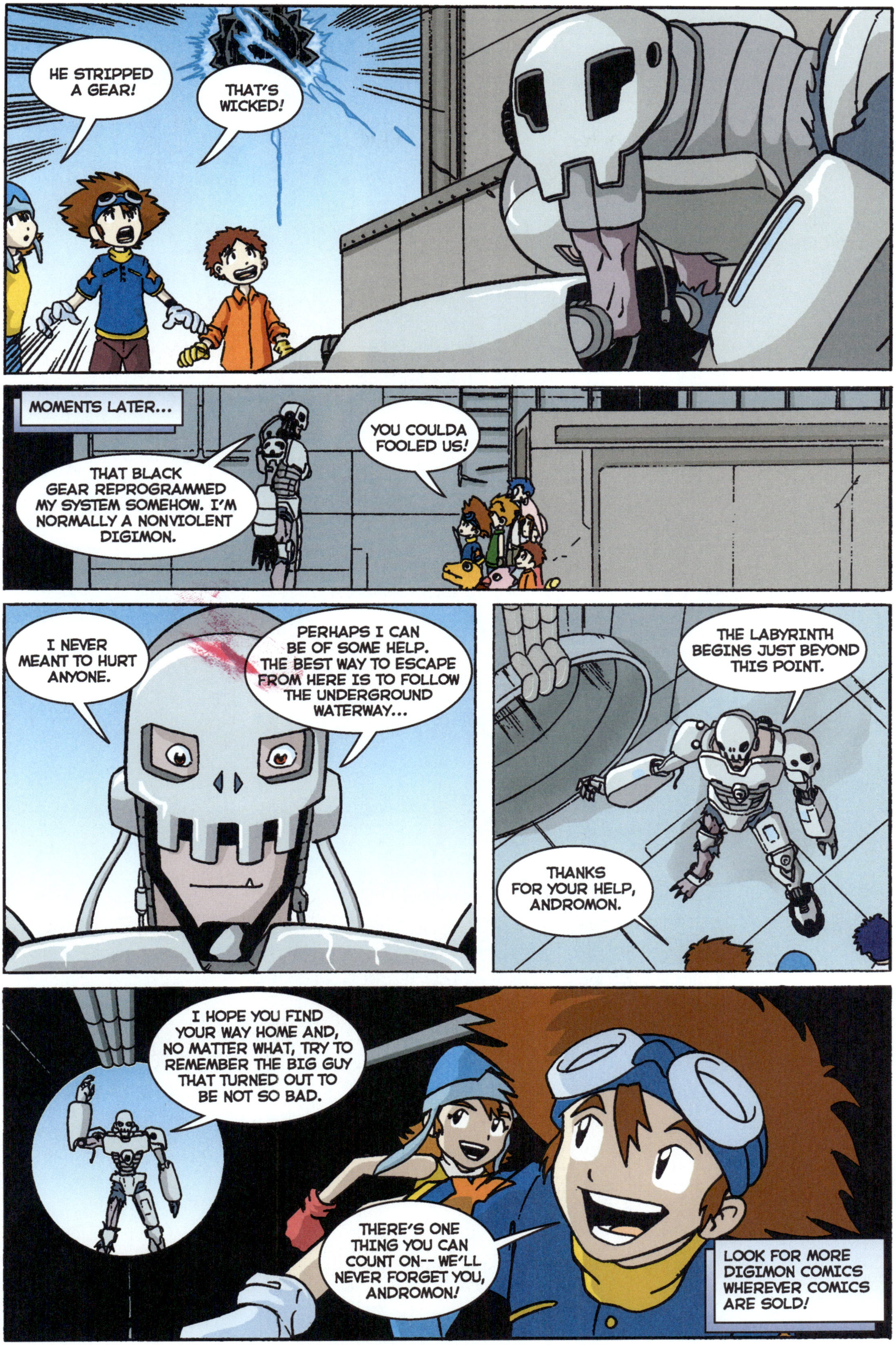
HE STRIPPED A GEAR!
THAT'S WICKED!
MOMENTS LATER...
THAT BLACK GEAR REPROGRAMMED MY SYSTEM SOMEHOW. I'M NORMALLY A NONVIOLENT DIGIMON.
YOU COULDA FOOLED US!
I NEVER MEANT TO HURT ANYONE.
PERHAPS I CAN BE OF SOME HELP. THE BEST WAY TO ESCAPE FROM HERE IS TO FOLLOW THE UNDERGROUND WATERWAY...
THE LABYRINTH BEGINS JUST BEYOND THIS POINT.
THANKS FOR YOUR HELP, ANDROMON.
I HOPE YOU FIND YOUR WAY HOME AND, NO MATTER WHAT, TRY TO REMEMBER THE BIG GUY THAT TURNED OUT TO BE NOT SO BAD.
THERE'S ONE THING YOU CAN COUNT ON-- WE'LL NEVER FORGET YOU, ANDROMON!
LOOK FOR MORE DIGIMON COMICS WHEREVER COMICS ARE SOLD!

Eek! STRAVAGANZA
FOX KIDS network
© & TM 1992
Fox Children's Network Inc.
KAT
ZZZZ
OUT OF THE WAY EEK, I WANT TO CUT THE GRASS
WHY SHOULD I....
AHHGG!... MOVE
NICE HAIRCUT EEK
I NEED A NICE BARBECUED STEAK AFTER THAT, NOW LET ME SEE - CHARCOAL, LIGHTING FUEL, MATCH...
BOOM
EVENTUALLY EEK GETS THE BARBECUE GOING
UH! UH! SMOKE!... I MUST DO SOMETHING
DON'T PANIC EEK, I'LL SOON HAVE THIS FIRE OUT!
MM98
THAT WAS A BIG MISTAKE
HEY SHARKEY, YOU DIDN'T MISS THE STEAK!

Eek! STRAVAGANZA
FOX KIDS network
© & TM 1992
Fox Children's Network Inc.
EEK SPOTS A UFO!
IT'S GOING TO LAND!
THEY'RE GETTING OUT OF THE SPACECRAFT
I COULD JUST HAVE A LITTLE LOOK AT IT!
LITTLE GREEN SPACECATS! CALL THE X FILES EEK
MMM... A CONTROL BOX, I WONDER WHAT THIS DOES...
EEK, DON'T PRESS THE.....
OOPS!
...RED BUTTON
EEK TRAVELS THROUGH SPACE....
... AND LANDS ON A DISTANT PLANET!
HI! I'M EEK, EEK THE CAT
WELCOME TO THE PLANET OF CATUTOPIA
YOU MUST BE HUNGRY AFTER YOUR JOURNEY, WE EAT THESE PILLS - THEY GIVE US ALL THE NOURISHMENT WE NEED!
WE LOVE YOU EEK
ON CATUTOPIA ALL IS HARMONY
THIS IS OUR MUSEUM, WE THINK OUR ANCESTORS ATE OUT OF THESE TINS, BUT WE DON'T KNOW HOW THEY OPENED THEM...
KITTY CATS
MM98
MY WORST NIGHTMARE, NO TIN OPENERS...
TO BE CONTINUED...

HOME TO RENT
STEREO
BUD
GORGIOUS
CANDY
ETNO
JUST TIME TO HANG OUT THE WASHING
TUM-TE-TUM
THAT'S IT. NOW WHERE'S THAT PROP?
TUT! WHY OH WHY DON'T PEOPLE PUT THINGS BACK WHERE THEY BELONG?
HM...NO CLOTHES PROP. WHAT CAN I USE INSTEAD?
JUST TURN ON THE GOLF AND COME BACK IN AN HOUR!
EXCELLENT! BUD'S BORED RIDGED!

HOME TO RENT
STEREO
BUD
GORGIOUS
CANDY
ETNO
CRACK
I'M GETTING IN SHAPE!!
YOU SHOULD TOO BUD
GOT MY NEW HEADBAND... GONNA DO SOME PRESS UPS
ONE
WHUMP!
NNGGHH!

HUM ALONE!
Ace Ventura & the Lost Treasure of the Stinkas!
Script: Mark Bennington Art: Nigel Parkinson Lettering: Gordon Robson
SOUTH AMERICA, THE TROPICAL MOUNTAIN REGION OF THE WRISTIES...
THE ANCIENT TRIBE OF THE STINCAS WORSHIPPED HALITOSIS – GOD OF BAD BREATH!
OH, DEITY OF DOG BREATH, PRINCE OF PONG, WE OFFER SWEET NECTAR TO SOOTHE YOUR MIGHTY MOUTH OF MOULDINESS!
THEY WERE GOB-FEARING PEOPLE!
GATHERED FROM OUR SACRED HUMMINGBIRDS...
EEEK! WE'RE DOOMED! THERE'S NO NECTAR!
'TIS WRITTEN IN THE ANCIENT PROPHECIES THAT THE MOTHER OF ALL STINKIES WILL ENGULF OUR LANDS IF WE ANGER THE MIGHTY HALITOSIS!
Sniff! Sniff! I, Er...THINK IT'S HAPPENING...
AIIEEEGH! THE GREAT SMELL IS UPON US!
PONGG!

DO NOT GO IN THERE! COULD I USE YOUR BATHROOM?
I'D JUST WRAPPED UP A CASE OVER MEXICO WAY WHEN DANGEDY-DANG, I LOST MY BEARINGS IN THE JUNGLE!
SO YOU ARE A DETECTIVE... THEN PERHAPS YOU CAN SOLVE OUR MYSTERY, MISTER VENTURA?!
FOR THE FIRST TIME IN CENTURIES, OUR SACRED HUMMINGBIRDS HAVE FAILED TO PROVIDE NECTAR!
HUMMINGBIRDS? REEHEEHEEHEEALLY?
"GEESE is the word is the word is the..."
"You're the SWAN that I want... Hoo Hoo HOOO!"
"You've got to PECK a pocket or two..."
THESE ARE NOT HUMMINGBIRDS... THEY CAN SING AND THEY KNOW ALL THE WORDS...
GASP!
SOME DIRTY DUDE HAS DUPED YOU BY SWITCHING YOUR HUMMING-BIRDS WITH BUDGERIGARS!

DON'T WORRY, CHIEF, I'LL SOLVE THIS MYSTERY IN NECTAR NO TIME AT ALL!
SEEDS, HUH?
Aha, MY HARE-IAL DETECT-HARE IS PICKING UP A FAINT SIGNAL...
HUMMMMMMMM
Gee, HUMTHING TELLS ME I'VE TRACKED DOWN THESE HUMMINGBIRDS!
HUMMMMMMMMM
HUM
SIZZLE
WHOOOAAAAA!
SPARK!
BZZZT
HEY, BUDDY! IT'S HOT ENOUGH OUT HERE WITHOUT YOU BARBECUING ON MY GENERATOR!*
BLERPSH!
* Warning: It is not advisable to try this at home - Spank you!

I'M PROFESSOR ANN TIQUITIES, ARCHAEOLOGIST – AND THIS IS MY ASSISTANT, DOCTOR ARTIE FACTS!
HOWDY DOODY DOO!
WHAAAGH!
FRIZZZ
TROWELS
BEANS
PEAS
MEXICAN BEANS
BEANS
PROFESSOR TIQUITIES HAS LOCATED THE FABLED "TIARA DEL FUEGO", THE VALUABLE GOLDEN HEADDRESS OF THE ANCIENT QUEEN OF THE STINCAS, WATTA HONKA.
AS YOU CAN SEE, MISTER VENTURA, THE TIARA IS TOTALLY INACCESSIBLE BY CLIMBING
IF THAT DARN CHOPPER HADN'T BROKEN DOWN, WE COULD HAVE EASILY HOVERED IN FOR THE TREASURE!
HOVER WITHOUT BOTHER– REEHEEHEEHEEALLY?
BIRD SEED SWEET & SOUR ANT FLAVOUR!
BUT MY FLIGHT CREW HAVE THE FLYING ABILITY OF A SACK OF POTATOES!
LOOK OUT BELOW!
WILBUR AND ORVILLE WRONG, THE PROF'S PILOTS, HAD A LOT TO LEARN ABOUT FLIGHT.
YOU BUNGLERS HAD BETTER COME UP WITH AN AIRCRAFT THAT CAN REACH THAT CLIFF INLET PRETTY SOON!
WE'RE WORKING ON IT, BOSS!

HOLY WATER, I'M SWEATING AMAZONS IN THIS TROPICAL HEAT!
SPLOOOOOSH!
ALRIGHTY, THEY'VE GOT TOWELS!
HEY, AMERICANO, GEET YOUR SWEATY, PEEGY FACE OUT OF MA' BEEST PONCHO!
AYE-EEE-AYE-EEE-YIPE!
KER POW!
APOLOGIES FOR MA' AMIGO PUNCHO. 'EEZ BEEN UN'APPY SEENCE 'EE CRACKED 'EEZ MARACAS THEEZ MORNING!
WELL, HE SHOULD STICK AN ATHLETIC CUP IN HIS PANTS!
THERE WAS SOMETHING PUZZLING ABOUT THE PONCHO'D PAN-PIPERS...
HOW DO THOSE GUYS STAY SO COOL? HAVE THEY GOT BUILT-IN AIR CONDITIONING?

A GREAT DETECTIVE ALWAYS PURSUES HIS ENQUIRIES WITH THE UTMOST PROFESSION-ALISM...
AZ-TEC!
HEY, YOU'RE NO GREAT SHAKES YOURSELF, BUTT-QUACK! DOCTOR DOODOO-BUNS! POOPY PANTS!
BLOW PIPE
ORNITHOLOGY
BIRD BOOK
THE TROWEL
NO, THAT VASE–IT'S AZTEC INDIAN–A RARE PIECE!
OOOPS! AS RARE AS THE TIARA DEL FUEGO, HUH?
OOH, THE TIARA IS A MILLION TIMES MORE VALUABLE THERE ARE MANY WHO WOULD DO ANY-THING TO GET THEIR HANDS ON IT!
IS THAT SO?
THE PROFESSOR'S HELICOPTER AROUSED MY SUSPICIONS...
SEEDS AGAIN?
DARTS ENOUGH MEDDLING, ACE VENTURA!
WOOOSH!
PYANG!
YEEOOOWCH! Gee... FEEL...KINDA...GROGGY...

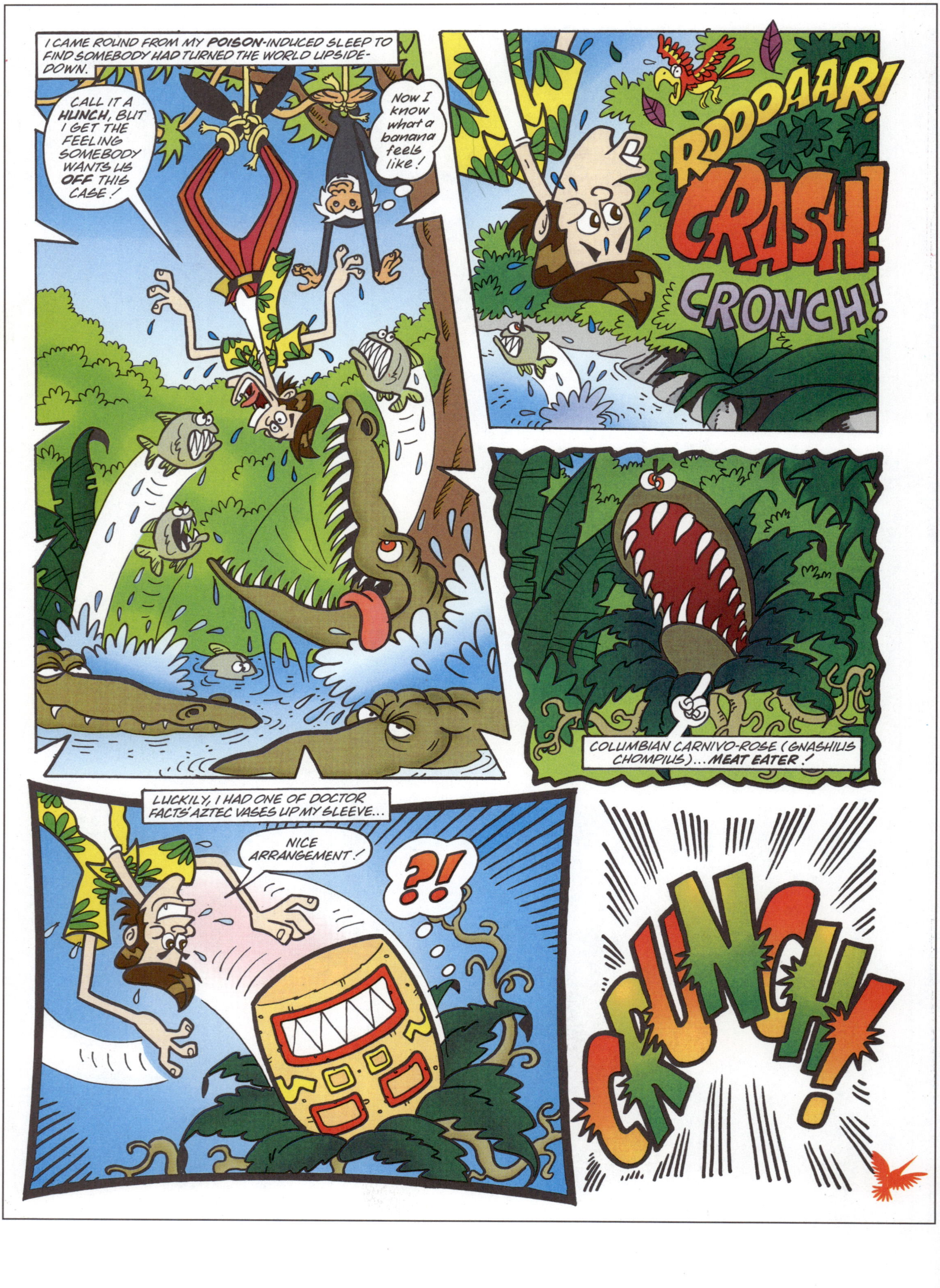
I CAME ROUND FROM MY POISON-INDUCED SLEEP TO FIND SOMEBODY HAD TURNED THE WORLD UPSIDE-DOWN.
CALL IT A HUNCH, BUT I GET THE FEELING SOMEBODY WANTS US OFF THIS CASE!
Now I know what a banana feels like!
ROOOAAR!
CRASH!
CRONCH!
COLUMBIAN CARNIVO-ROSE (GNASHIUS CHOMPIUS)... MEAT EATER!
LUCKILY, I HAD ONE OF DOCTOR FACTS' AZTEC VASES UP MY SLEEVE...
NICE ARRANGEMENT!
?!
CRUNCH!

HECK, WHAT WAS THAT WE JUST HIT?
WE'RE GOING DOWN AGAIN!
SHE'S OUT O' CONTROL, WILBUR!
UP! PULL HER UP!
AAAGGH!!
CRASH!
PRANG!!
OH, SHUCKS! BACK TO THE DRAWING BOARD!
Y'KNOW, WE SHOULD REALLY LEARN A THING OR TWO FROM OUR FEATHERED FRIENDS!
1 TON LLAMA OOH-NASTY EXTRA SMELLY
SOFT LANDING... SPANKS A HEAP, BUDDY!

I HAD SEEN ENOUGH TO KNOW THAT THE HUMMINGBIRD HAUL WAS IN THE LIGHT-FINGERED HANDS OF SOME-ONE IN THIS CAMP...
FRAGILE
ARTIFACTS
FARTI-FACTS
PROFESSOR ANN TIQUITIES
WILBUR & ORVILLE WRONG
PANCHO
PUNCHO
DOCTOR ARTIE FACTS
PAUNCHO
CAN YOU FIND THE FIEND THAT FILCHED OUR FEATHERED FRIENDS?
Did you note down the clues that can nick the nesty nasty? For the sake of HUManity and HUMming Rights, liberty and justice, you'd better get it right, alrighty?...

SOON ZEE WEALTH OF ZEE TIARA WILL BE OURS, AMIGOS!
Heh, heh! READY FOR TAKE-OFF?
NECTAR
GO, GO, LEETLE BIRDIES, Ha-haaa!
GEE, WHAT TOOK YA?
VENTURA, HOW DEED YOU GEET 'ERE?
I FIGURED YOU PONCHOS WERE THE PINCHOS... PANCHO'S CRACKED MARACAS DROPPED SEEDS AT THE CRIME SCENES...
YOU WERE TOO COOL IN THIS HEAT, HAVING THE BIRDS UNDER YOUR HATS, THEIR RAPIDLY BEATING WINGS ACTED AS AIR CONDITIONING...
YOU USED YOUR HAT FEATHERS TO DART ME IN THE JUNGLE — IN FACT, YOUR PANPIPES MADE A GREAT SIX-SHOOTER BLOWPIPE...
AND LASTLY, I SAW PAUNCHO COLLECTING INSECTS TO FEED YOUR CAPTIVES!
PHEW-WOO! DID YOU FEEL THAT, HUH?
YOU'RE GOING DOWN, PANCHO!
SNAP! SNAP! SNAP! SNAP!
AAIEE! YOU CRAZY AMERICANO, YOU'LL KEEL UZ ALL!
Uh-oh!

NEXT MONTH: The Highland fling - Ace style!

FOX KIDS network
Eek! STRAVAGANZA™
© & TM 1992
Fox Children's Network Inc.
EEK IS ON THE PLANET CATUTOPIA
PILLS FOR FOOD, FRIENDLY MICE, NO TIN OPENERS! URGH... I'VE GOT TO GET HOME!
SO EEK SNEAKS OFF TO THE SPACECRAFT ...
AND HEADS FOR HOME!
EARTH
BACK ON EARTH...
WELCOME BACK EEK, YOU'VE MISSED ALL THE FUN, THE ALIEN CATS HAVE BEEN TELLING US ABOUT THEIR WONDERFUL PLANET
THEY ARE GOING TO SHOW US HOW TO ALL LIVE IN HARMONY, NO MORE COOKING ... JUST EAT LITTLE PILLS... GREAT EH ......
I CAN SEE THE FUTURE, ...NO TIN OPENERS! I'VE GOT TO DO SOMETHING...
WOULD YOU GUYS HAVE A QUICK LOOK AT YOUR SPACECRAFT, I HAD A LITTLE BUMP WITH AN ASTEROID ON MY WAY BACK!
THE HYPERDRIVE THINGY IS A BIT WONKY!
SEEMS FINE TO ME
CONTROL BOX!
EEK PRESSES THE CONTROL AND ....
... SENDS THE ALIENS HOME!
IT'S A SHAME, THEY COULD HAVE GIVEN US SO MUCH.
DON'T WORRY, I'VE GIVEN THEM SOMETHING TO TAKE BACK....
ACME TIN OPENER

HOME for RENT
STEREO
BUD
GORGIOUS
CANDY
ETNO
EXCUSE ME GORGIOUS!
HUH!
ARE YOU AWARE OF THE RELATIVE VISCOSITY OF MUCAL EFFLUENT...
...WHEN APPLIED TO A MODERATELY TEXTURED VERTICAL SURFACE?
NOT REALLY!
FURTHER MORE, ARE YOU SENSIBLE OF THE TIME FRAME INVOLVED UNTIL SUCH SUBSTANCES BIODEGRADE?
UR...
NOPE!
WELL STOP STICKING BOGIES ON THE TOILET WALL THEN!!?!??!!

SABAN'S POWER RANGERS LOST GALAXY

EPIC BATTLES

For the first time in many years, the Earth is at peace. Thanks to the tireless work of the Power Rangers, led by the wise and gentle Zordon and then the beautiful Dimitria, the world has been saved from a series of wicked villains intent on destroying it. First there was Rita Repulsa whose evil tricks almost overcame the Rangers. Then came Lord Zedd, Rita's boss, who attacked with an army of hideous monsters. When Rita and Lord Zedd marry and are joined by Rita's brother, the forces of evil were only just kept at bay. Next there was a new threat, King Mondo and Queen Machina, who elbowed the other villains aside and unleashed their awful robot army upon the world. Only the power of the Zeo Crystals gave the Rangers a fighting chance here. And when Rita on one side and the Machine Empire on the other finally destroyed each other, up stepped the terrible space pirate, Divatox, the worst threat of all. Only the mighty Turbo Zords gave the Rangers enough firepower to defeat their deadliest foe.

THE NEW CHALLENGE

All these mighty battles are now history. With the world safe, a special city called Terra Venture can be built inside a massive spaceship. It will be launched to find another planet where humans can live.

Meanwhile, however, the power of evil is raising its ubly head in another part of the universe. In a far-off galazy, a tyrant called Scorpius attacks a peaceful jungle tribe led by a clever girl called Maya. The villain wants five famous swords, the Quaser Sabers, whose blades were stuck in a huge stone thousands of years ago.

During the attack by scorpius, a black hole appears and Maya finds herself transported through it. She lands on Terra Venutre and tells her plight to the four teenagers on board. Vowing to helo Maya, they set off to do battle with Scorpius. But they do not realise his power and are on the verge of defeat when they pull the Quaser Sabers free and turn into the Power Rangers. Now the battle is really on!

Furious at being defeated, Scorpius turns the whol of Maya's planet to stone and the Rangers are forced to retreat back to Earth through the black hole. Unaware that their enemy and his band of vicious Generals have followed them, determined to gain the Sabers, the Rangers set off on their journey through the unecplored reaches of Space. Their greatest battles are yet to come...

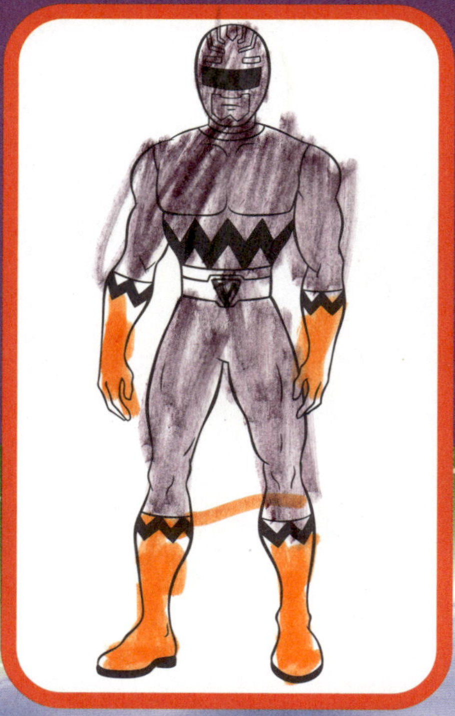

Colour these pictures of the Power Rangers, using the image above to guide you

HEROES AND VILLIANS

- Daring and sport loving, LEO is the RED POWER RANGER. His powers of quick decision-making also make him the leader.
- Joker DAMON is the GREEN POWER RANGER. A great mechanic and a good boxer, his skills prove very useful to the rest of the team.
- KENDRIX, highly intelligent and scientific, is the PINK POWER RANGER. Her growing friendship with Leo also teaches her the importance of emotions.
- The BLUE POWER RANGER is KAI, a sensible and straightforward young man with a strict army background. He would like to lead the Power Rangers.
- MAYA, the girl whose planet was turned to stone, is proud to be the YELLOW POWER RANGER. Happier in the jungle than in the city, Maya is determined to overcome Scorpius and restore the life to her world.

FOX KIDS ™

SPIDER-MAN

JACK O'LANTERN

REAL NAME:
JASON PHILIP MACENDALE JR

PLACE OF BIRTH:
BOSTON, MASSACHUSETTS

OCCUPATION:
ASSASSIN

HEIGHT:
6' 1"

BACKGROUND:
An ex-CIA operative turned bad guy, Jack O'Lantern combines his deadly skills with the latest high tech weaponry available. He is a well known assassin who has developed a personal grudge against Spider-Man following several defeats at the web-slinger's hands.

MYSTERIO

REAL NAME:
QUENTIN BECK

PLACE OF BIRTH:
RIVERSDALE, CALIFORNIA

OCCUPATION:
FORMER SPECIAL EFFECTS DESIGNER AND STUNTMAN

HEIGHT:
5' 11"

BACKGROUND:
Following a failed career in the movies, Beck chose to use his abilities to kill Spider-Man. His powers are all driven by his skills to create illusions and special effects but these serve to make him one of the trickiest of Spidey's foes. Reality and fantasy often merge when Mysterio attacks.

foe file

MORBIUS
THE LIVING VAMPIRE

REAL NAME: DR MICHAEL MORBIUS

PLACE OF BIRTH: EASTERN EUROPE

OCCUPATION: SCIENTIST AND VAMPIRE

HEIGHT: 6'1"

BACKGROUND:
Michael Morbius was a Nobel prize winning scientist, who realised he was dying from a rare blood disease. During an experiment to cure himself using the blood of vampire bats, an electric shock altered Morbius' body, turning him into a living vampire!

Kingpin

REAL NAME: WILSON FISK

PLACE OF BIRTH: UNKNOWN

OCCUPATION: CRIMELORD

HEIGHT: 6' 7"

BACKGROUND:
The Kingpin has used his intelligence and strength to take over the mob operations of New York. Ruthless in his pursuit of power, various shady business deals have put him beyond the law. No other criminal is as powerful or successful as Fisk, who is the true Kingpin of crime.

KRAVEN THE HUNTER

REAL NAME: SERGEI KRAVINOV

PLACE OF BIRTH: RUSSIA

OCCUPATION: HUNTER AND ADVENTURER

HEIGHT: 6'4"

BACKGROUND:
Kraven comes from an ancient line of Russian nobility and has been trained from birth to be the best hunter in the world. A mysterious serum granted him great speed and strength. Spider-Man is the only prey he has hunted to have escaped alive.

LIZARD

REAL NAME: DR CURT CONNORS

PLACE OF BIRTH: CORAL GABLES, FLORIDA

OCCUPATION: SCIENTIST

HEIGHT: 5' 11"

BACKGROUND:
When Dr Connors was researching ways of recreating missing limbs, he used a special serum taken from the DNA of lizards on himself. While it restored his own missing arm it also changed him, turning him into the savage and brutal monster known only as The Lizard!

IF YOU ASK ME, YOU'RE JUST THE GUYS TO GET GIFT-WRAPPED...
WAY TO GO SPIDER-MAN!
SPIDEY-STYLE!
HELP US CLEAR THIS TIP, WEB-HEAD - OR THE KID GETS IT!
WAAK!
IF THERE'S ONE THING I CAN'T STAND, IT'S A BULLY!

WOW, MRS PARKER - YOU'RE ALMOST AS COOL AS SPIDER-MAN!
NOW NOW, DEAR. I DON'T WANT YOU TO THINK VIOLENCE IS A GOOD THING.
WHY, IF MY PETER WAS HERE, I'M SURE IT COULD'VE ALL BEEN SORTED OUT WITHOUT RESORTING TO FISTICUFFS!
PETER PHONED THE POLICE, MRS PARKER. I'M SURE HE'LL BE HERE SOON.
WHAT DO YOU MEAN - DEFEATED!?
I PROMISED MY WIFE, VANESSA, THAT I WOULD CEASE MY CRIMINAL ACTIVITIES AT MIDNIGHT, TURK.
I NEED THAT HOSPITAL CLEARED BY THEN!
GET ME THE SINISTER SIX!
THUMPP!

AND SO...
YA GOTTA BE KIDDIN'. AIN'T YOU HEARD - IT'S CHRISTMAS!!
AND THE SANDMAN ALWAYS SPENDS CHRISTMAS WITH HIS MOM!
YOU WOULD HAVE KRAVEN ATTACK A FOE AT CHRISTMAS? NEVER!
WHERE WOULD BE THE THRILL OF THE CHASE, THE NOBILITY OF THE HUNT?
BESIDES, AUNTIE YELTSIN'S SENT ME SOME CHRISTMAS CAKE OVER.
I'VE JUST WON SECOND PRIZE IN A FANCY DRESS PARTY - AND TOMORROW WE'RE HAVING A BIG MEAL. THE VULTURE'S LIFE OF CRIME IS AT AN END.
AT LEAST UNTIL BOXING DAY.
IT'S NO USE. ALL THE OTHERS ARE IN JAIL OR ON HOLIDAY. THERE'S NO WAY I CAN GET THE SINISTER SIX TOGETHER...
UNLESS I FORM MY OWN SINISTER SIX...

LATER...
THANKS FOR HELPING SERVE THE MEALS, PETER. THESE POOR ORPHANS HAVE NOWHERE ELSE TO GO...
OKAY, EVERYONE. DON'T SAY THE BOSS DIDN'T WARN YOU.
LEAVE NOW - OR I'LL SET THE SINISTER SIX ON YOU!
THIS IS OUR PARTY AND YOU'RE NOT INVITED!
YEAH, YOU SMELL!
OKAY, YOU BRATS, YOU ASKED FOR THIS.
Trapster
Vanisher
Doughboy
The Living Brain
Toad
THE NOT-SO-SINISTER SIX
HA HA, I THINK YOU MEAN THE NOT-SO SINISTER SIX!
THERE'S ONLY FIVE, ARE YOU STUPID OR SOMETHING?

I'M THE SIXTH MEMBER!
GET THEM, MY FEROCIOUS FRIENDS.
WHAM!
I'D HARDLY CALL THEM FEROCIOUS.
STUPID, DAFT AND SOON-TO-BE DEFEATED BUT DEFINITELY NOT FEROCIOUS.
THIS IS FUN!
GET HIM!
I CAN'T WAIT TO MEET THE LOSER WHO ARRANGED ALL THIS!

NEVER LET A FOOL DO A MAN'S JOB, SPIDER-MAN!
I THOUGHT EVEN TURK COULD TAKE CARE OF SUCH A MINOR JOB AS INTIMIDATION.
SMASH!
IT SEEMS THAT I WAS WRONG!
HEY, I DID MY BEST. HAVE YOU TRIED GETTING HOLD OF GOOD BAD GUYS AT CHRISTMAS?
I WAS LUCKY TO EVEN GET THIS BUNCH OF LOSERS.
SAY BUDDY, WHO'RE YOU CALLING A LOSER!?
I CALCULATE HE IS IN TROUBLE!

CLEANING OUT A HOSPITAL'S LOW EVEN FOR YOU, KINGPIN - WHAT'S THE DEAL?
IF THIS HOSPITAL IS EMPTIED BY CHRISTMAS DAY I CAN BUY IT CHEAP, TEAR IT DOWN AND BUILD A CASINO IN ITS PLACE!
BUT THESE CHILDREN, THEY'RE SICK. THEY HAVE NOWHERE ELSE TO GO!
YUK!
UUMPH!
LIKE I CARE!

LIFE IS HARD. LIFE IS PAIN.
BOING!
THE SOONER THE LITTLE WHELPS REALISE THAT THE BETTER!
HAPPY CHRISTMAS, WEB-SLINGER. PREPARE TO DIE!
GET YOUR HANDS OFf HIM, YOU BIG BULLY. HE'S MY FRIEND!
WHY, YOU INSOLENT BRAT. I'LL...
WILSON, DEAR, IS THERE A PROBLEM?
STOP FIGHTING, IT'S THE KINGPIN'S WIFE.

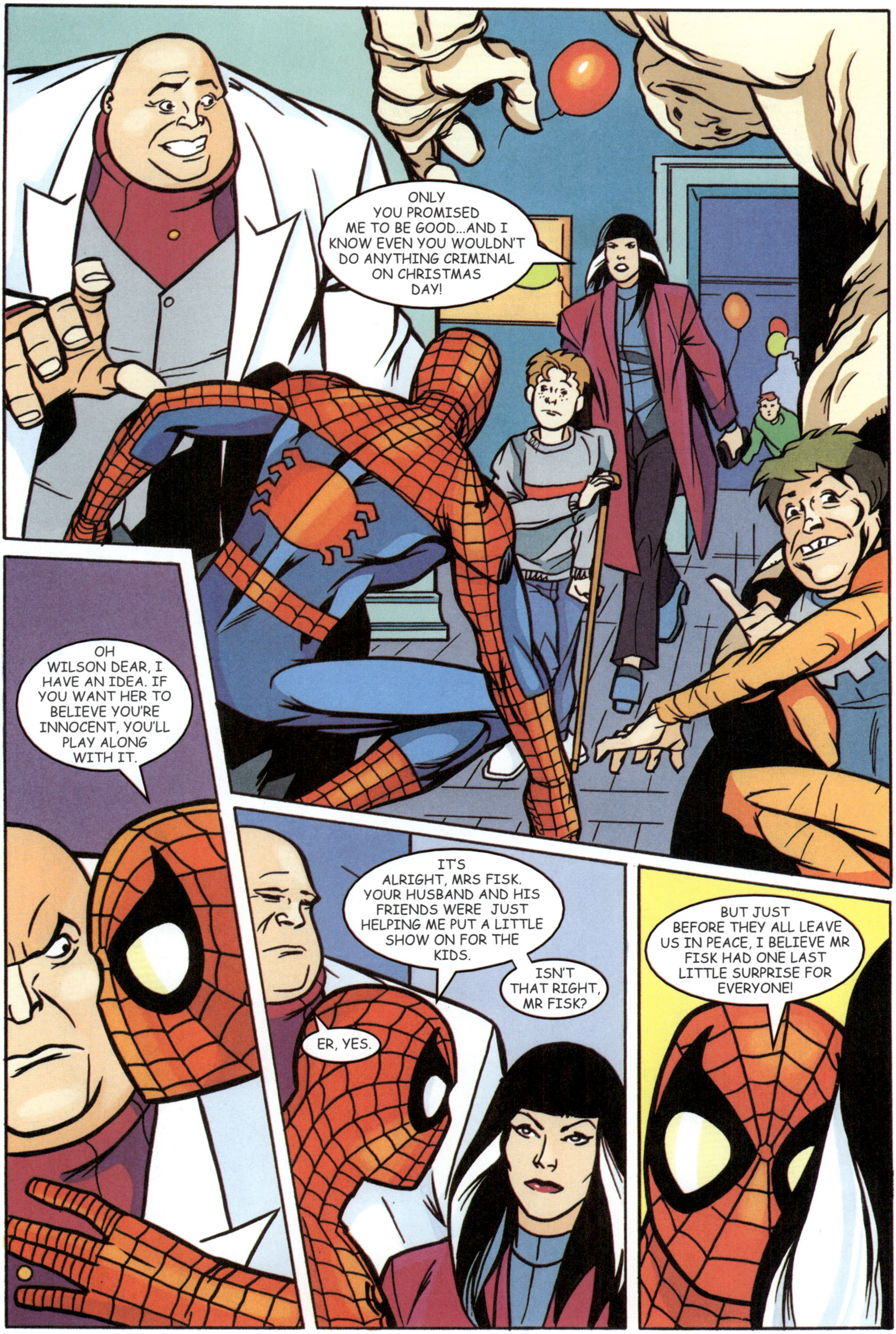
ONLY YOU PROMISED ME TO BE GOOD...AND I KNOW EVEN YOU WOULDN'T DO ANYTHING CRIMINAL ON CHRISTMAS DAY!
OH WILSON DEAR, I HAVE AN IDEA. IF YOU WANT HER TO BELIEVE YOU'RE INNOCENT, YOU'LL PLAY ALONG WITH IT.
IT'S ALRIGHT, MRS FISK. YOUR HUSBAND AND HIS FRIENDS WERE JUST HELPING ME PUT A LITTLE SHOW ON FOR THE KIDS.
ISN'T THAT RIGHT, MR FISK?
ER, YES.
BUT JUST BEFORE THEY ALL LEAVE US IN PEACE, I BELIEVE MR FISK HAD ONE LAST LITTLE SURPRISE FOR EVERYONE!

I'LL GET YOU FOR THIS, SPIDER-MAN!
HA HA, HAPPY CHRISTMAS EVERYONE!
SAY, WHAT HAPPENED TO THE VANISHER?
HE, ER... VANISHED!
THE END.

FOX KIDS network
Eek! STRAVAGANZA™
© & TM 1992
Fox Children's Network Inc.
THE KIDS ARE TAKING EEK ON HOLIDAY ...
SUNSKY BREAKS
WE MUST MAKE A LIST OF ESSENTIAL THINGS TO PACK, TRY TO KEEP IT TO A MINIMUM ! - AND EEK, DON'T FORGET YOUR SWIMMING COSTUME.
ONE OF THE GREAT MYSTERIES OF LIFE... WHY DO CARTOON ANIMALS, WHO NEVER WEAR CLOTHES, ALWAYS HAVE TO PUT ON COSTUMES TO GO SWIMMING ?
Surfboard
BMX
Skateboard
Walkman
Snorkle
Football
Ball caps
sunglasses
Sport Shirts
- Villa
- Spurs
- Arsenal
- England
- Home
- Away
FOX
Make up
Sun cream
Hair spray
Shampoo
Camera
Sterio
CD's
Shoes
Dresses
Tops
Jeans
Shorts
Skirts
EEK, IS THAT ALL YOUR TAKING ?
YOU DID SAY ONLY ESSENTIALS !
Tin Opener

HOME TO RENT
STEREO
BUD
GORGIOUS
CANDY
ETNO
SNIFF
WHAAA!!
WHAT'S THE MATTER BUD?
OH DARLING
HM! BUD APPEARS TO BE WATCHING AN ANCIENT MONOCHROME MOVING IMAGE
OH! MUST IT END LIKE THIS?
WEETABIX... ...WEEK...AH! HERE IT IS... WEEPY
...A ROMANTIC CELLULOID FILM IN WHICH TWO HUMANS WHO ARE ONLY BLACK & WHITE ARE FORCED BY CIRCUMSTANCES TO PART FOR EVER, USUALLY ON A STEAMY RAILWAY PLATFORM.
IS THAT WHAT IS MAKING YOU CRY BUD?
NO! THIS STUPID FILM HAS REPLACED MY LEARNING ZONE COURSE... POND SCUM FOR BEGINNERS!!

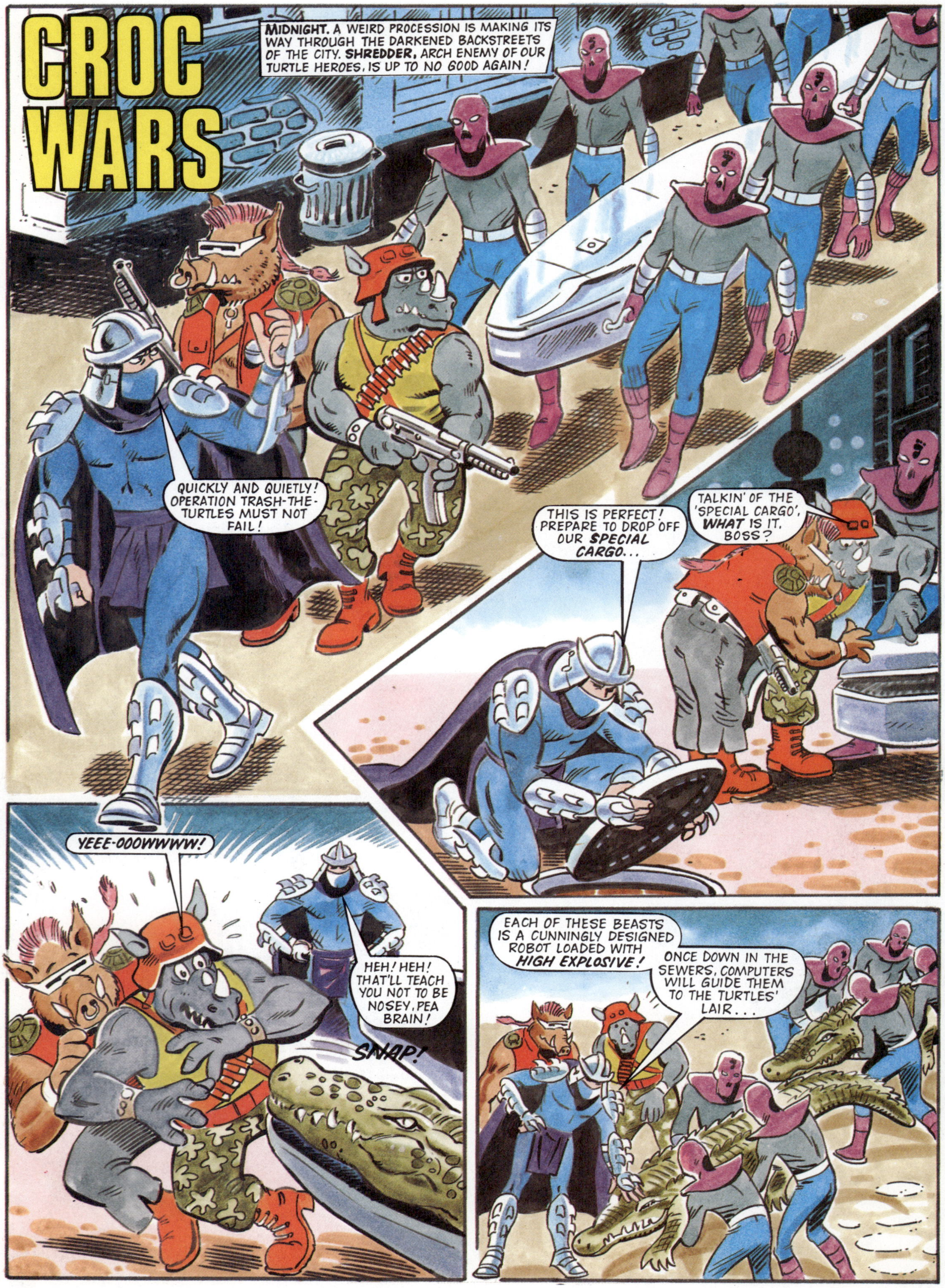
CROC WARS
MIDNIGHT. A WEIRD PROCESSION IS MAKING ITS WAY THROUGH THE DARKENED BACKSTREETS OF THE CITY. SHREDDER, ARCH ENEMY OF OUR TURTLE HEROES, IS UP TO NO GOOD AGAIN!
QUICKLY AND QUIETLY! OPERATION TRASH-THE-TURTLES MUST NOT FAIL!
THIS IS PERFECT! PREPARE TO DROP OFF OUR SPECIAL CARGO...
TALKIN' OF THE 'SPECIAL CARGO', WHAT IS IT, BOSS?
YEEE-OOOWWWW!
HEH! HEH! THAT'LL TEACH YOU NOT TO BE NOSEY, PEA BRAIN!
SNAP!
EACH OF THESE BEASTS IS A CUNNINGLY DESIGNED ROBOT LOADED WITH HIGH EXPLOSIVE!
ONCE DOWN IN THE SEWERS, COMPUTERS WILL GUIDE THEM TO THE TURTLES' LAIR...

...AND THEN BOOM!
ONE WAY
SHREDDER AND HIS GOONS. LUCKY I DID THE LATE NEWS TONIGHT...
SCREEECH!
I DON'T KNOW WHY THEY'RE STUFFING CROCS DOWN DRAINS, BUT I'LL GET IT ON VIDEO ANYWAY...
SHREDDER! IT'S THAT TURTLE LOVIN' REPORTER, APRIL O'NEIL!
SHE COULD WRECK ALL MY PLANS... GRAB HER!
TIME TO LEAVE, I THINK... OOOPS!
THAT'S AS FAR AS YOU GO, LADY!
YEAH, AND YOU WON'T BE NEEDIN' THE CAMERA AGAIN!
THE TURTLES ARE UNAWARE OF APRIL'S CAPTURE...
HMMM! THIS IS THE LIFE... MUNCHING AWAY ON PIZZA AND CUSTARD!
I PREFER THE OLD FAVOURITE, JELLY AND PIZZA...

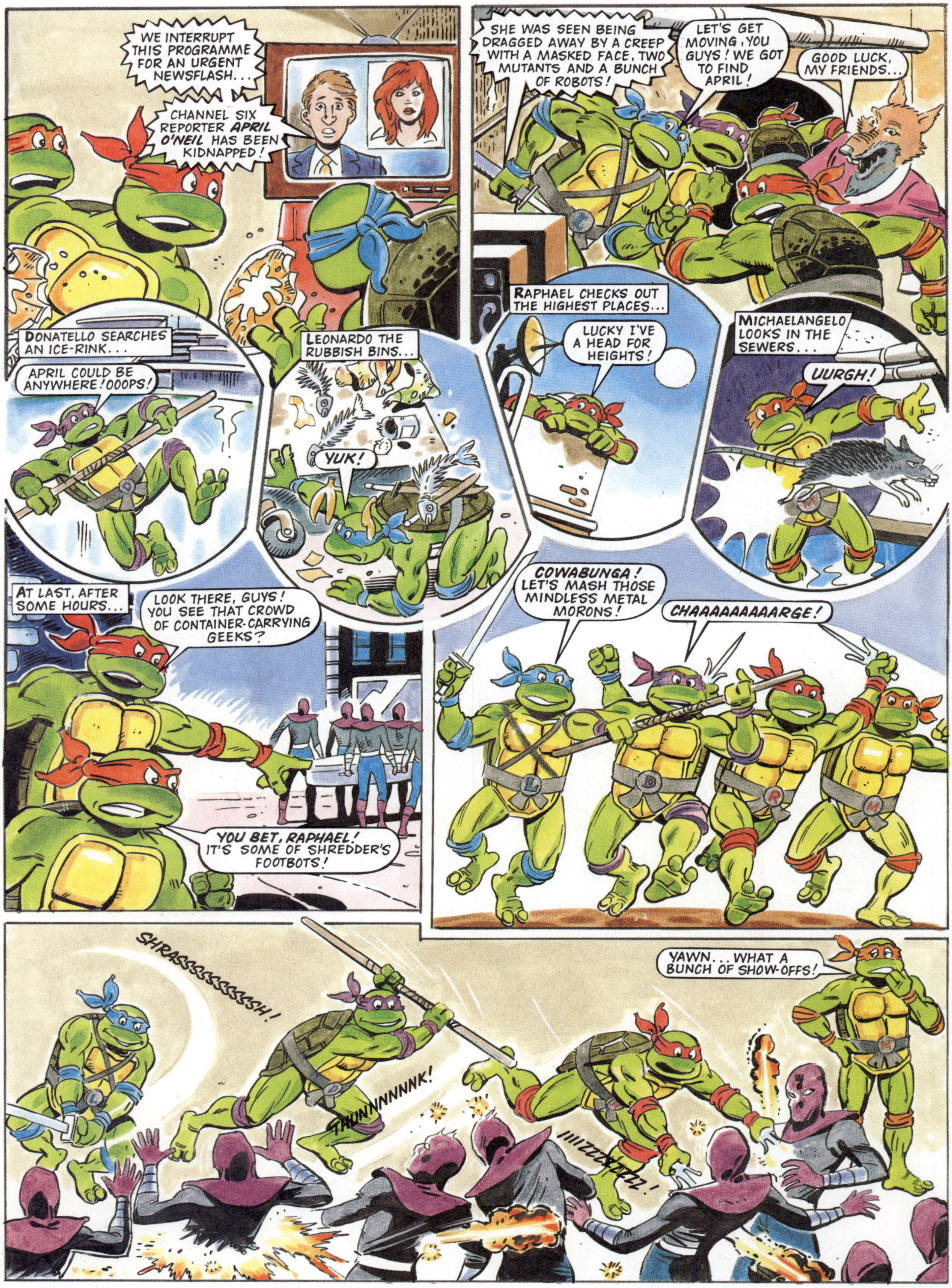
WE INTERRUPT THIS PROGRAMME FOR AN URGENT NEWSFLASH...
CHANNEL SIX REPORTER APRIL O'NEIL HAS BEEN KIDNAPPED!
SHE WAS SEEN BEING DRAGGED AWAY BY A CREEP WITH A MASKED FACE, TWO MUTANTS AND A BUNCH OF ROBOTS!
LET'S GET MOVING, YOU GUYS! WE GOT TO FIND APRIL!
GOOD LUCK, MY FRIENDS...
DONATELLO SEARCHES AN ICE-RINK...
APRIL COULD BE ANYWHERE! OOOPS!
LEONARDO THE RUBBISH BINS...
YUK!
RAPHAEL CHECKS OUT THE HIGHEST PLACES...
LUCKY I'VE A HEAD FOR HEIGHTS!
MICHAELANGELO LOOKS IN THE SEWERS...
UURGH!
AT LAST, AFTER SOME HOURS...
LOOK THERE, GUYS! YOU SEE THAT CROWD OF CONTAINER-CARRYING GEEKS?
YOU BET, RAPHAEL! IT'S SOME OF SHREDDER'S FOOTBOTS!
COWABUNGA! LET'S MASH THOSE MINDLESS METAL MORONS!
CHAAAAAAAAARGE!
SHRASSSSSSSSSSH!
YAWN... WHAT A BUNCH OF SHOW-OFFS!
THUNNNNNNK!
IIIIZZZZZZZ!

OL' MICHAELANGELO PREFERS TO USE HIS HANDS!
DAAAAAAAANG!
AND THEN THERE WERE NONE! THAT WAS SHORT AND SWEET...
UH-HUH, LEO, BUT US TURTLES ARE SHORT AS WELL...
...SHORT BY ONE!
DONATELLO'S DISAPPEARED!
HEH, HEH! NONE OF THOSE TURTLE WIMPS SAW US SNEAK UP AND GRAB THEIR BUDDY!
TOO BAD FOR THEM! LET'S GET HIM BACK TO THE TECHNODROME BEFORE HE COMES TO...
LATER, AT SHREDDER'S SINISTER BASE...
EVENIN', LADY! FEELIN' A LITTLE LONELY?
NOT FOR YOUR COMPANY, YOU RHINO-FACED FREAK!
SHAME! IN THAT CASE, HERE'S ONE OF YOUR TURTLE PALS!
DONATELLO! WHAT HAVE THEY DONE TO YOU?

SIGH... I'LL BE OKAY IN A MINUTE, APRIL... OR MAYBE TEN!
BUT TIME'S RUNNING OUT! SHREDDER'S SENT A FLEET OF EXPLOSIVE-CARRYING ROBO-CROCS TO BLOW RAPHAEL AND THE OTHERS INTO THE MIDDLE OF NEXT WEEK!
WHY DIDN'T YOU SAY SO?
COME ON! THERE MUST BE SOMETHING HERE WE CAN USE TO SEND A WARNING TO THE REST OF THE GUYS!
MEANWHILE, A MISERABLE TRIO OF TURTLES RETURN TO THE SEWERS...
MICHAELANGELO, MY SON, YOU LOOK EXHAUSTED... AND MUCH SADDENED!
WE ALL ARE... WE'VE FOUND NO SIGN OF EITHER APRIL OR DONATELLO...
THEN YOU MUST REST! A TIRED TURTLE CAN SO EASILY BECOME A DEAD TURTLE!
THE FIRST CROCODILE IS IN POSITION! VICTORY, AT LAST, IS MINE...
BUZZZZ
BLEEEEEP
...FAREWELL AND GOOD RIDDANCE, MY VILE GREEN ENEMIES!
WH-WHAT'S HAPPENING? AAGGGHHHH!
IT IS THE END... AAYYIIIHH!
IN THE TECHNODROME, DONATELLO AND APRIL ARE WORKING QUICKLY...
WELL, IT'S NOT THE BEST LOOKING RADIO I'VE EVER MADE, BUT I RECKON IT WILL WORK!
HAVING A SCIENTIFIC GENIUS AROUND IS ALWAYS USEFUL! FINGERS CROSSED THEN...
HEY! STOP FOOLIN' WITH THAT JUNK, TURTLE... SHREDDER WANTS YOU!
HUH? NOT NOW, YOU STUPID MUTANT ...I'M BUSY!

TOUGH LUCK! YOU'RE COMIN' WITH US, READY OR NOT!
S-SORRY, APRIL... HERE'S WHERE YOU TAKE OVER!
OH, BROTHER...
HOPE THAT'S RIGHT! IF THIS DOESN'T WORK, THE TURTLES ARE YESTERDAY'S NEWS...
MAYDAY! EMERGENCY! THIS IS APRIL O'NEIL CALLING THE TURTLES!
UUUUHH... M-MICHAELANGELO HERE... THAT... THAT YOU, APRIL...
RIGHT ON! GET MOVING FAST! YOU'VE A BUNCH OF EXPLODING CROCODILES CLOSING IN!
TEN-FOUR!
SLEEPING TIME'S OVER, GUYS! IT'S TIME FOR ACTION WITH A CAPITAL 'A'!
DO...DO YOU HAVE TO SHOUT, MIKE?
TURTLE AND RAT ATTACK!
HAI! PREPARE TO TEAR THESE KILLERS APART, MY SONS...
YOU SAID IT, MASTER...
GOTCHA!
SO LONG, DUDE!
BUTT OUT, CROC!
THWAAAAAK!
HAI-SAI!
ZAAAAAAAAAP!
BACK AT THE TECHNODROME...
I DON'T UNDERSTAND! ALL CONTACT WITH THE CROCS HAS BEEN LOST!
LOOKS LIKE YOUR PLANS HAVE GONE DOWN THE DRAIN YET AGAIN, CREEP!

IT WAS THE O'NEIL WOMAN! SHE SENT A WARNIN' TO HER FRIENDS!
ACE GOING, APRIL! I KNEW YOU COULD DO IT!
GRAAAHH! I SHALL HAVE MY REVENGE... ANNIHILATOR ROBOT, DESTROY THEM!
YIKES! I... I GUESS WE JUST RAN OUT OF LUCK!
RELAX, DONATELLO! APRIL TOLD US WHERE YOU WERE BEING HELD!
SPLINTER... THE TURTLES... NO!
HAAAAAAAI!
I HATE HEROES! I'M GONNA WASTE YOU ALL!
QUICKLY, DON, TAKE THIS...
GNNNHH!
AND IT'S GOODNIGHT FROM HIM!
THEY HAVE WON. I MUST SAVE MY-SELF...
UNNNK!
SHREDDER HAS FLED, MY SONS, AND WE SHALL DO THE SAME!
UH-HUH, THE TURTLES HAVE A HQ TO REBUILD... BUT I RECKON WE CAN LEAVE THAT TO APRIL AND DONATELLO!
HAA, HAA... YOU'RE JOKING... I HOPE!
END

Eek! STRAVAGANZA
© & TM 1992
Fox Children's Network Inc.
EEK AND THE KIDS ARE STAYING IN A SEASIDE CARAVAN
IT'S YOUR TURN TO DO THE LAUNDRY AND IRONING, WE ARE OFF TO THE BEACH
BUT I WANTED TO GO WATER SKIING TODAY...
HMMPH... WASHING IRONING... GRRR...
IDEA!
ISN'T THAT EEK OUT THERE ?

HOME TO RENT
STEREO
BUD
GORGIOUS
CANDY
ETNO
DON'T SAY I DIDN'T WARN YOU!
SLAM!
AAAAARRRGHHH!!
HUH?
PTOO!
YOU DIDN'T NEED THAT MUCH CHILLI POWDER THEN!

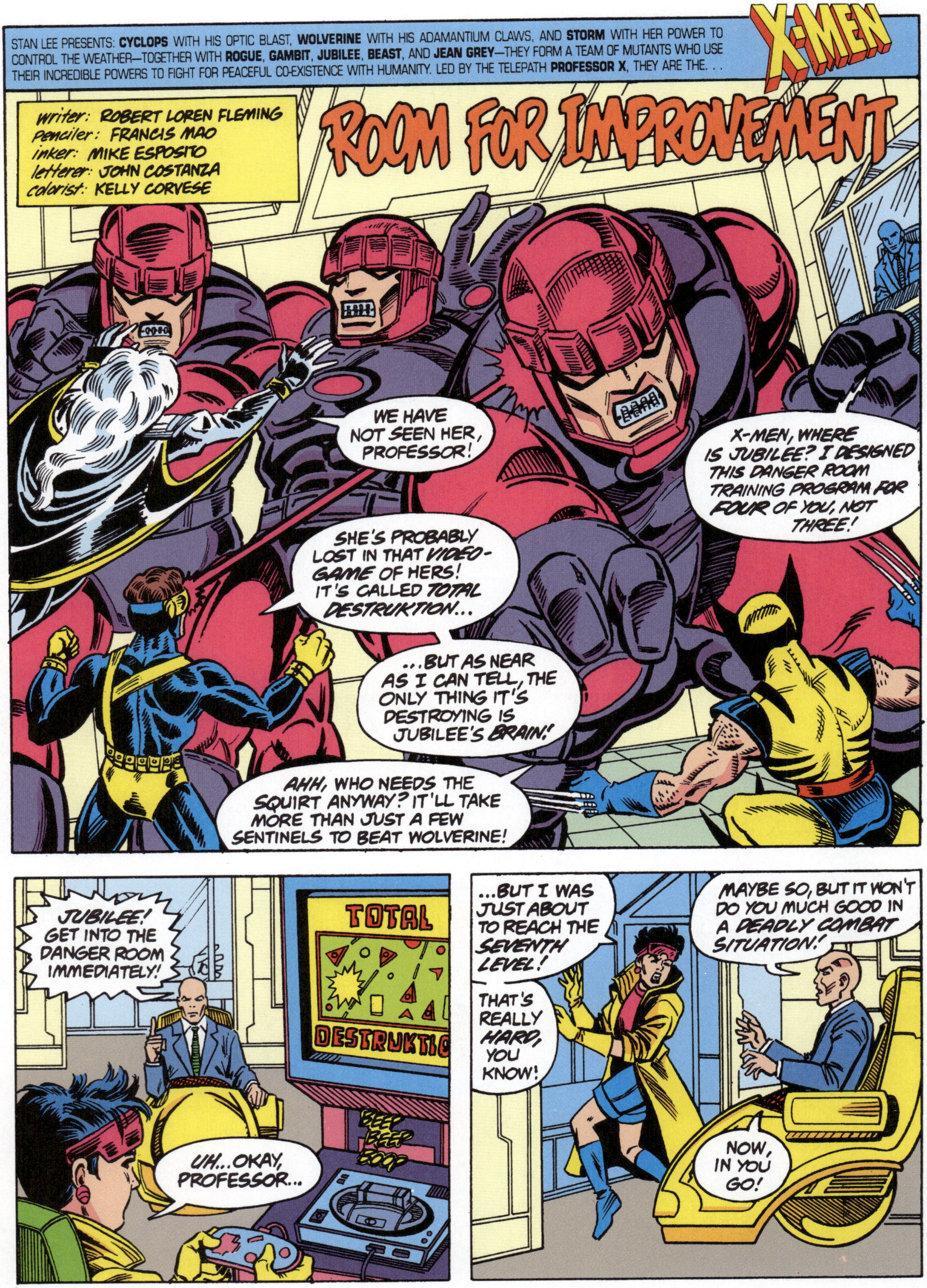

STAN LEE PRESENTS: CYCLOPS WITH HIS OPTIC BLAST, WOLVERINE WITH HIS ADAMANTIUM CLAWS, AND STORM WITH HER POWER TO CONTROL THE WEATHER—TOGETHER WITH ROGUE, GAMBIT, JUBILEE, BEAST, AND JEAN GREY—THEY FORM A TEAM OF MUTANTS WHO USE THEIR INCREDIBLE POWERS TO FIGHT FOR PEACEFUL CO-EXISTENCE WITH HUMANITY. LED BY THE TELEPATH PROFESSOR X, THEY ARE THE. . .
X-MEN
ROOM FOR IMPROVEMENT
writer: ROBERT LOREN FLEMING
penciler: FRANCIS MAO
inker: MIKE ESPOSITO
letterer: JOHN COSTANZA
colorist: KELLY CORVESE
X-MEN, WHERE IS JUBILEE? I DESIGNED THIS DANGER ROOM TRAINING PROGRAM FOR FOUR OF YOU, NOT THREE!
WE HAVE NOT SEEN HER, PROFESSOR!
SHE'S PROBABLY LOST IN THAT VIDEO-GAME OF HERS! IT'S CALLED TOTAL DESTRUKTION...
...BUT AS NEAR AS I CAN TELL, THE ONLY THING IT'S DESTROYING IS JUBILEE'S BRAIN!
AHH, WHO NEEDS THE SQUIRT ANYWAY? IT'LL TAKE MORE THAN JUST A FEW SENTINELS TO BEAT WOLVERINE!
JUBILEE! GET INTO THE DANGER ROOM IMMEDIATELY!
TOTAL
DESTRUKTIO
BEEP BEEP BOOP
UH...OKAY, PROFESSOR...
...BUT I WAS JUST ABOUT TO REACH THE SEVENTH LEVEL!
THAT'S REALLY HARD, YOU KNOW!
MAYBE SO, BUT IT WON'T DO YOU MUCH GOOD IN A DEADLY COMBAT SITUATION!
NOW, IN YOU GO!

SHE HAS SPUNK, THAT ONE! WITH A BIT MORE DISCIPLINE, SHE'D--
--HUH?!
THE DOOR TO THE CONTROL ROOM--CLOSING ON ITS OWN! I'M LOCKED OUT!
MUST HURRY TO THE VIEWPORT!
WITHOUT ACCESS TO THE CONTROL ROOM I CAN'T CONTROL THE DANGER ROOM PROGRAMS.
STILL, EVERYTHING SEEMS NORMAL SO FAR...
WATCH ME KNOCK THIS SENTINEL OFF-BALANCE WITH A PLASMA BLAST, CYCLOPS!
GOOD WORK, JUBILEE!
NOW I'LL BRING IT ALL THE WAY DOWN WITH AN OPTIC BLAST!
NICE TOUCH, STORM--
AND I'LL FREEZE IT TO THE FLOOR WITH AN INSTANT ICE STORM!
--BUT THE ONLY GOOD SENTINEL IS A PERMANENTLY DESTROYED SENTINEL!
SKWARRK

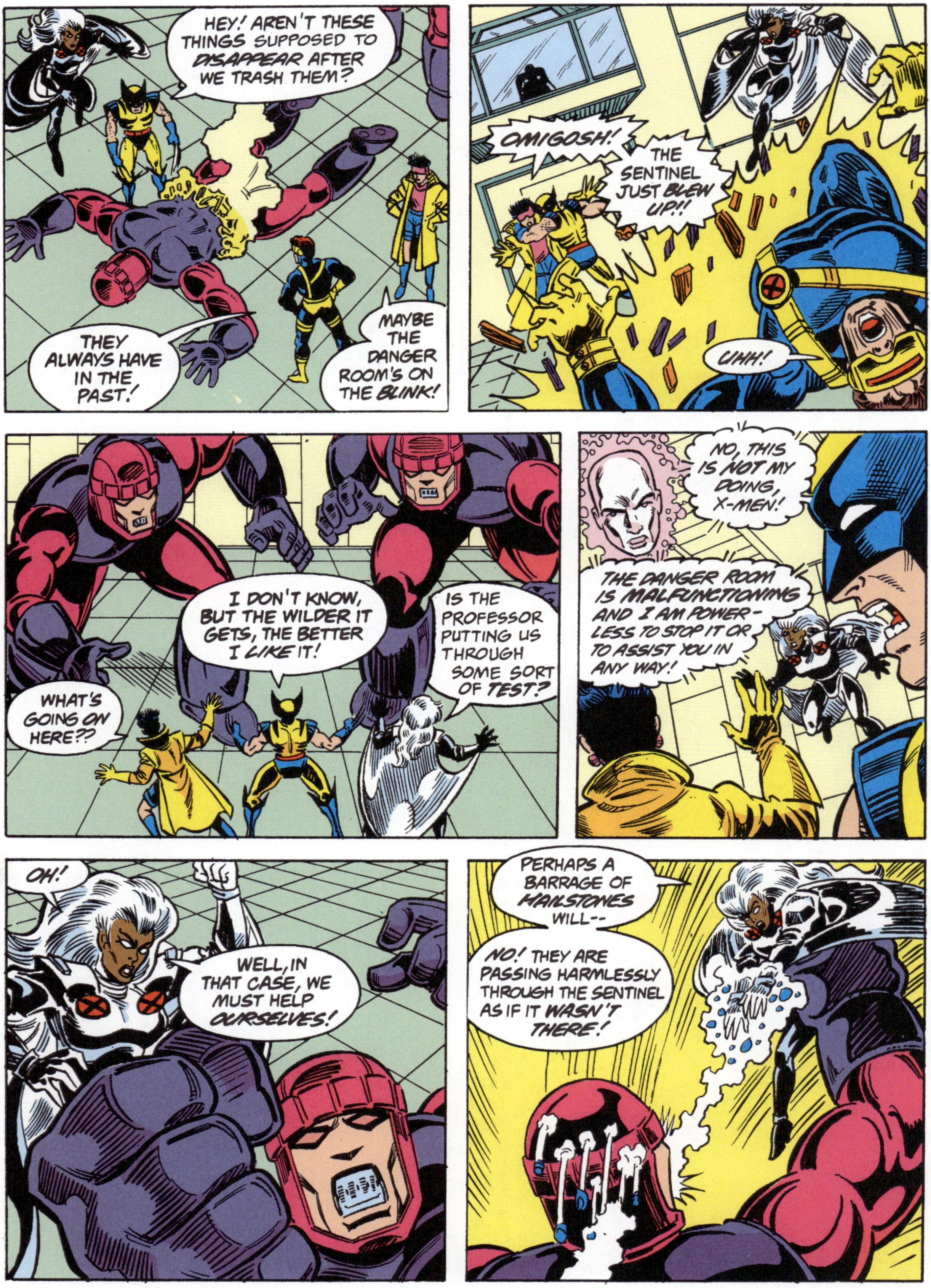
HEY! AREN'T THESE THINGS SUPPOSED TO DISAPPEAR AFTER WE TRASH THEM?
THEY ALWAYS HAVE IN THE PAST!
MAYBE THE DANGER ROOM'S ON THE BLINK!
OMIGOSH!
THE SENTINEL JUST BLEW UP!!
UHH!
I DON'T KNOW, BUT THE WILDER IT GETS, THE BETTER I LIKE IT!
IS THE PROFESSOR PUTTING US THROUGH SOME SORT OF TEST?
WHAT'S GOING ON HERE??
NO, THIS IS NOT MY DOING, X-MEN!
THE DANGER ROOM IS MALFUNCTIONING AND I AM POWER-LESS TO STOP IT OR TO ASSIST YOU IN ANY WAY!
OH!
WELL, IN THAT CASE, WE MUST HELP OURSELVES!
PERHAPS A BARRAGE OF HAILSTONES WILL--
NO! THEY ARE PASSING HARMLESSLY THROUGH THE SENTINEL AS IF IT WASN'T THERE!

STORM'S PASSED OUT!
WE'VE GOT TO HELP HER!
GET THAT THING, WOLVIE!
I DON'T TAKE ORDERS FROM YOU, SQUIRT, BUT I'LL BE GLAD TO WRECK THIS BUCKET OF BOLTS ALL THE SAME!
NUTS! MY CLAWS PASSED RIGHT THROUGH IT AS IF IT WAS A GHOST!
CLANG!
WHOA!
GREAT! WE CAN'T LAY A FINGER ON THESE SENTINELS, BUT THEY HAVE NO TROUBLE KICKING THE STUFFING OUT OF US!
HOW THE DEVIL DO YOU STOP SOMETHING YOU CAN'T TOUCH, BUT THAT CAN TOUCH YOU??
GASP
WOLVERINE! THAT'S THE VERY PROBLEM THAT WAS STOPPING ME FROM REACHING THE SEVENTH LEVEL OF TOTAL DESTRUKTION!!
CAN THE DANGER ROOM HAVE SOMEHOW TURNED INTO A REAL-LIFE VERSION OF MY VIDEO-GAME?
THAT IS PRECISELY WHAT HAS HAPPENED, CHILD! A COMPUTER VIRUS FROM YOUR GAME CARTRIDGE MUST HAVE INFECTED THE DANGER ROOM PROGRAM...
OH, NO!
...AND IF YOU CAN'T FIGURE OUT HOW TO REACH THE SEVENTH LEVEL, YOU AND YOUR TEAMMATES ARE DOOMED!

THINK, KID, THINK!
BLAM
BELIEVE ME, I'M TRYING!
CLUNK!
CLUNK!
IF ONLY I HAD SOME CLUE...
WAIT A MINUTE... THAT'S IT!
SEVENTH LEVEL, HERE I COME!
SNAP!
READERS-- DID YOU SPOT THE CLUE THAT JUBILEE NOTICED IN THE PREVIOUS PANEL?
WOLVIE, FOLLOW MY LEAD AND DO EXACTLY WHAT I TELL YOU!
OKAY, KID... BUT I HOPE YOU KNOW WHAT YOU'RE DOING!
THE ANSWER IS SO SIMPLE, I'M SURPRISED I DIDN'T THINK OF IT BEFORE!
IT CAME TO ME WHEN I NOTICED TWO CHUNKS OF DEBRIS BOUNCING OFF THOSE SENTINELS...
SPAKK
...WHICH MEANS THEY BECOME SOLID IF THEY'RE BOTH HIT AT THE EXACT SAME TIME! LIKE--
--NOW!!
HEY, YOU'RE RIGHT! MY CLAWS ARE BACK IN BUSINESS!
KREEESH!

DON'T LET UP ON THEM!
IF THEY SEPARATE, IT'LL BE HARDER TO COORDINATE OUR ATTACKS!
LOOK, THEY'RE WEAKENING!
IF WE CAN JUST KEEP UP THE ASSAULT FOR A FEW MORE SECONDS...
YOW!
YOU DID IT, KID!
CONGRATULATIONS, YOU HAVE REACHED THE SEVENTH LEVEL! GAME OVER!
CHECK IT OUT! THE DOORS ARE OPENING!
DANGER'S PAST, STORM! UP AND AT 'EM!
YOU OKAY, CYCLOPS?
JUST SORRY TO HAVE MISSED THE ACTION, JUBILEE!
WELL, DON'T LOOK NOW, CYKE--
gasp
--BUT YOU JUST MIGHT GET A SECOND CHANCE!
WOULD YOU LIKE TO PLAY AGAIN?
WE ARE OUTTA HERE!!
THE END

'the

FOX KIDS™

information games chat

penpals

horoscopes

news

competitions

chat

Hook up with keyboard tappers around the planet and stay in touch, Your inbox never need be empty again! Who knows who'll be dropping in any minute?

fox kids boutik

Pop in anytime. There'll always be new stuff - toys, games, sweets and branded merchandise are all available for kids that save their brix.

briX

See something you want, click on the picture and the computer will grab the brix out of your wallet and send you the goody, if it's still in stock.

Easy!

www.foxkids.co.uk

reviews

books, music, film, dvd & video, games, shows, toys, cool stuff - check out what's new!

place to hang out online"

entertainment community boutik

jukebox

treasure hunt

wallet

brix

Keep the brix you earn on this site locked up safely with your own online wallet!
The more you play around the site, the more brix you'll rack up, the bigger the prize you can trade them in for! You can check how many brix you've got at any time.

games

games

my homepage

Building your own homepage couldn't be easier. Just follow the guide on the site and you'll have a top site in no time!

<www>

ecards

Forget someone's birthday? Wanna cheer someone up? Maybe you just feel like saying Hi!

Why not send a cool e-card?

vote

Tell us what you think... and help us to feature the coolest things on the site.

agony uncle

downloads